Thomas John Capel

Catholic

An essential and exclusive attribute of the true Church. Fourth Edition

Thomas John Capel

Catholic
An essential and exclusive attribute of the true Church. Fourth Edition

ISBN/EAN: 9783337000165

Printed in Europe, USA, Canada, Australia, Japan

Cover: Foto ©Lupo / pixelio.de

More available books at **www.hansebooks.com**

"CATHOLIC:"

An Essential and Exclusive Attribute of

the True Church,

BY

Right Revd. Monsignor CAPEL, D. D.

FOURTH EDITION.

NEW YORK:

Wilcox & O'Donnell Co., Publishers, 131 William St.

D. & J. Sadlier & Co., 31 Barclay St.

1884.

BY THE SAME AUTHOR:

CONFESSION AND ABSOLUTION. *2d Edition.*

———————

THE POPE : To which is added the Propaganda Question.

In preparation.

"CATHOLIC:"

An Essential and Exclusive Attribute of the True Church.

BY

RIGHT REVD. MONSIGNOR CAPEL, D. D.

Domestic Prelate of His Holiness, Leo XIII., happily reigning,
Member of the Roman Congregation of the Segnatura,
Priest of the Archdiocese of Westminster.

"Christianus mihi nomen est; Catholicus vero cognomen." S. Pacien, A. D. 373.

FOURTH EDITION.

NEW YORK:
WILCOX & O'DONNELL Co., PUBLISHERS, 131 William St.

D. & J. SADLIER & Co., 31 Barclay St.
1884.

TO THE MEMBERS

OF THE PROTESTANT EPISCOPAL CONVENTION,

HELD AT PHILADELPHIA IN THE YEAR OF GRACE 1883,

AND TO THOSE WHOM THEY REPRESENTED,

IS THIS LITTLE WORK DEDICATED

BY THEIR SERVANT IN XT,

THE AUTHOR.

CHRISTIANUS MIHI NOMEN EST; CATHOLICUS VERO COGNOMEN:

ILLUD ME NUNCUPAT, ISTUD OSTENDIT;

HOC PROBOR, INDE SIGNIFICOR.*

* St. Pacien, Bishop of Barcelona
A. D. 373.

Arno, Cal., June 10, 1904.

Editor Freeman's Journal:

Dear Sir — I have just read with much interest your article on "Catholic or Roman Catholic." Thinking it might interest readers, I send you a pamphlet of mine where the question is treated from pages 111 to 117, which you may like to reproduce in the pages of your excellent New York Freeman's Journal.

Yours very respectfully,

T. J. CAPEL.

PREFACE.

The God of Truth cannot have revealed contradictory doctrines. Sects proclaiming contradictory doctrines cannot all be right, though all may be wrong. In like manner the same essential attribute cannot be predicated in the same sense of two religious societies having fundamentally different principles of belief and of worship.

"Catholic" was decreed to be a note of the Christian Church fifteen hundred years ago by its teachers assembled in General Council.

"The Protestant Episcopal Church" in the United States created in the year 1789, now lays claim to the name Catholic. But this is already in the possession of the Roman Church. To try and establish who is the lawful possessor, is the object of this little work.

The importance of the issue will be seen from the following passage written by St. Cyprian, Bishop of Carthage, no less than fifteen hundred and thirty years ago.

"The Church is likewise one, though she be spread abroad, and multiplies with the increase of her progeny; even as the sun has rays many, yet one light; and the tree boughs many, yet its strength is one seated in the deep-lodged root; and as, when many streams flow down from one source, though a multiplicity of waters seem to be diffused from the bountifulness of the overflowing abundance, unity is preserved in the source itself. Part a ray of the sun from its orb, and its unity forbids the division of light; break a branch from the tree, once broken it can bud no more; cut the stream from its fountain, the remnant will be dried up. Thus the Church, flooded with the light of the Lord, puts forth her rays through the whole world, with yet one light, which is spread upon all places, while its unity of body is not infringed. She stretches forth her branches over the universal earth, in the riches of plenty, and pours abroad her bountiful and onward streams ; yet is there one head, one source, one mother abundant in the results of her fruitfulness. . . . Whoever parts company with the Church and joins himself to an adultress, is estranged from the promises of the Church. He who leaves the Church of Christ attains not Christ's rewards. He is an alien, an outcast, an enemy. He can no longer have God for a Father who has not the Church for a Mother."

Calm, honest investigation of the matter cannot be other than an olive branch of peace, leading prayerful, earnest souls into the Ark of Salvation.

For the advantage of those who have not a library of the Fathers, there have been appended the Treatise of St. Cyprian on the Unity of the Church written in 251; the eighteenth of the Catechetical Instructions of St. Cyril of Jerusalem, written in 347, and the letter of St. Pacien, Bishop of Barcelona, on the name Catholic, written in 373.

It is thought these treatises, of a dogmatic nature, representing Africa, Asia Minor, Western Europe, and emanating from Saint Bishops of the " Undivided Church," will prove to be voices to which a deaf ear will not be turned. The Oxford translations have for obvious reasons been selected.

To these authors have been added the strong opinion of Lord Macaulay. His words have weight inasmuch as he, a Protestant, sees in the Roman Catholic Church, merely a human Body Politic.

Pentecost-day, 1884.

New York.

PART I.

THE ARGUMENT.

CATHOLIC:

AN ESSENTIAL AND EXCLUSIVE ATTRIBUTE OF THE TRUE
CHURCH.

The Protestant Episcopal Church held its Convention, in
October last, at Philadelphia. While in session, among other
questions discussed, was that of changing the title of the
Book of Common Prayer "according to the use of the Protestant Episcopal Church in the United States of America."
It was proposed that the words "Protestant Episcopal" be
struck out, and that in lieu thereof, the words "Holy Catholic" be inserted. To this was made an amendment, to
suppress "Protestant Episcopal" and merely leave "The
Church."

The amendment was lost. The original motion was then
put and was defeated by 252 nays against 21 yeas. This
decision of the House of Deputies, sitting as Committe-
tee of the whole House, together with a report thereon
was carried to the House of Bishops. Their Lordships decided, in face of the vote, that it was inexpedient to alter
the title page of the Book of Common Prayer.

The discussion was animated, and was marked, as is usual
whenever any Protestant sect holds an assembly, by sundry
thrusts at the "errors of the Roman Catholic Church," or as
one of the speakers described it "that foreign body which
impudently called itself the Catholic Church." However
painful such assertions may be, they ought not to warp the
judgment, or lessen the charity and interest of those who

sincerely believe in the Master's words: "Other sheep I have that are not of this Fold, them also I must bring, and they shall hear my voice, and there shall be one Fold and one Shepherd."[1]

That in the representative body of the Protestant Episcopalians, there should have been found one-twelfth of its members claiming the name, "Catholic," for their religious Society, is a remarkable sign of the times, and one worthy of the most earnest consideration.

It has increased importance if there be added the undeniable fact that the so-called High Church movement has gained a sure footing, and is making steady progress among the Protestant Episcopalians. The doctrines of the Sacrifice of the Mass, of the Real Presence of Jesus in the Blessed Sacrament, of Confession and Priestly Absolution, of prayers and honor to the Saints, more especially to the Queen of Saints: are now more or less openly taught in a number of the Episcopalian Churches."[2]

Why the teachers and believers in such doctrines do not

---

1 St. John X. 16.

2 While passing this work through the press, the following appeared in the New York *Herald* of May 5th: " This Church of ours, said the new pastor of St. Ignatius, Fortieth street, in this city, is the Catholic, and there is a vast difference between the spirit of the Catholic Church and the spirit of Protestantism. In the Protestant Church the all-important factor of successful work is the personal power of the minister, but in the Catholic Church it is the faithful ministering of the means of grace that gives our power."

In speaking of auricular confession and the sacrifice of the mass, he said: " What we believe of the blessed Sacrament is that in it the Son of God is present in the very flesh which he took of the Virgin Mary, His mother, and in the very blood which He pours out so freely for us upon the cross, and we believe that he will abide there under the sensible form of bread and wine as long as this world shall last. And of the confessional, we believe that our auricular confession is a part of the preaching of God's ministers. I should be unfaithful to my trust if I held back from proclaiming by my words and by my practice that confession is necessary to salvation, and that God's ministers have the power to forgive sins."

return to the Old Church, seeing that these were the very doctrines repudiated at the so-called Reformation, as the Thirty-nine Articles and the Book of Homilies shew, is to any intelligent mind inexplicable.

Naturally with belief in these doctrines, have come practices which were unknown to the Episcopalians of the past generations ; such as reservation of the sacrament, auricular confession, the use of vestments, ritual, confraternities of the Blessed Sacrament and of the Blessed Virgin, processions, blessings of palms, and many other practices, some of which are in plain language, devotions generated in the Roman Church in the last few centuries. In like manner our books of piety and Catholic works on the spiritual life even of the post-reformation period are, after excision and adaptation, appropriated by the High Church party.

There is no city of any size in the States where such religious belief and practices have not a fair, sometimes even a large following. And if the descriptions of the press be accurate the conformity with Roman Catholic liturgy and doctrines is complete.[1]

Of those who do believe and so practise, the greater number are verily convinced their Church is not Protestant but Catholic. They are in simple honest faith; they act with good conscience, and accordingly they receive of God grace, and joy, and peace.

This memorable movement, begun some forty-five years

---

1 *Vide* the local papers of the next morning on the last Palm Sunday and Good Friday services in St. Clement's Church, Philadelphia.

ago in the Established Church of England, has been the means of turning the minds of many to the Faith of their Forefathers, to the belief in a Sacramental System, to sounder knowledge of the great truths of the Christain religion, to more accurate ideas concerning the Church and Church authority, to the proper administration of baptism, to some idea of the Christian Altar and Sacrifice and above all to a truer knowledge of the Incarnation.

If in half a century so great a change has been brought about where protestant bigotry was rampant, what may not be expected in the next generation of those who will succeed the present holders of High Church teaching, many of whom are now validly baptized.

Personally I feel that God's providence created, and is directing the movement, and that it is leading souls unconsciously but none the less certainly to the One Fold under the One Shepherd. And in venturing to treat the question "Catholic : an essential and exclusive attribute of the True Church," I am anxious to contribute, however modestly, to advancing the movement to its true goal—the One Holy Catholic Apostolic and Roman Church.

In doing this I have no contentious or controversial spirit. And when it was suggested in November last, by the public press that I was to make an attack on the Protestant Episcopalians, I felt it wiser to postpone till later the publication of the question now to be treated. Unity of mind and heart is far more easily produced by frank explanation than by heated contention. Many misunderstandings would

disappear if men would state precisely their respective posi-
tions.

To do so in this case it is proposed to treat in outline :
(i) of the nature of the Church ; (ii) of the true idea of
Catholicity; (iii) of the formation of the Anglican Communion ; (iv) of the Protestant Episcopal Church in America.

1.

,It is of paramount importance that a clear idea be obtained of the nature of the Church of Christ. Of the sacred
writers, one only, St. Paul defines the Church. Writing to the
Colossians the Apostle says : "He (Christ) is the *Head* of
the Body, the Church," and in the same Epistle : "I fill up
those things that are wanting of the sufferings of Christ in
my flesh for *His Body which is the Church."* To the Ephesians he writes still more explicitly : "He hath put all things
under his feet, and hath made Him *Head* over *all the Church
which is His Body* and the fulness of him who is filled all in
all." ² In each instance St. Paul writes in the Greek language which has not the figurative expression Body; nor is
Body used therein ambiguously as it is in English. The
Apostle whenever he so defines the Church, invariably selects
the word σῶμα which is never used in Greek to express
mere association, or aggregation, but usually implies the
superadded idea of an organism. The full meaning of St.
Paul will be realized in the passage given above from the

---

(1), Eph. i, 23. (2), 2 Colossians i, 18 and 21.

Ephesians, where Christ is described as the "Head" in which κεφαλή is used, as the context shows, not merely in the sense of chief, but as the source of life to this Organism, His Mystical Body.

What the Apostle so accurately defines, he as vividly describes, and always in the same sense. Having stated the purposes for which the Church exists, St. Paul continues : "But performing the truth in charity we may in all things grow up in Him who is the *Head*, Christ : from whom the whole *Body* compacted and fitly joined together, by what every joint supplieth, according to the operation in the measure of every part, making increase of the *Body* unto the edifying itself in charity." [1].

" No man," says the same Apostle, " ever hated his own flesh ; but nourisheth and cherisheth it, as Christ doth the Church ; for we are members of His body, of His flesh, and of His bones." [2]. And therefore to the Galatians is he able to write : " " For as many of you as have been baptized in Christ, have put on Christ. There is neither Jew nor Greek ; there is neither bond nor free ; there is neither male nor female. For you are all ONE in Christ Jesus." [3]. And in similar strain does St. Paul address the Romans : "For as in one body we have many members, but all the members have not the same office : So we being many are one *Body* in Christ, and each one members one of another." [4] And to the Corinthians does he express this even more explicitly:

1, Eph. iv, 15.   2, Eph. v, 29.   3, Gal. iii, 27.   4, Rom. xii., 4.

"For as the body is one and hath many members, and all the members of the body whereas they are many, yet are one body; so also in Christ. For in one spirit were we all baptized into one *Body*. . . . God hath tempered the body together, giving the more abundant honor to that which wanted it, that there might be no schism in the body, but the members might be mutually careful one for another. And if one member suffer anything all the members suffer with it ; or if one of the members glory all the members rejoice with it. Now you are the *Body* of Christ and members of member. And God indeed hath set some in the Church, first apostles, secondly prophets, thirdly teachers, after that miracles, then the graces of healings, helps, governments, kinds of tongues, interpretations of speeches." [1].

These plain declarations of St. Paul shew that he regarded the Church as a Visible and Organic Body, divinely constituted with organs having their special functions, and receiving life through the Head, Christ. The minute description given in the fourth chapter of the Ephesians puts this beyond doubt.

The Apostle therein begins by a very precise statement of the unity which obtains: " ONE BODY, and One Spirit; as you are called in one hope of your calling ; one Lord, one Faith, one Baptism; one God and Father of all, who is above all, and through all, and in us all." He then enumerates the several parts of the Organism: "And some

---

1 1 Cor· xii., 12-28,

He gave to be apostles, and some prophets, and others evangelists, and others pastors and teachers." He specifies the
purpose for which the power is conferred: (1) "for the perfect-
ing of the saints," (2) "for the work of the ministry," (3) "for
the edifying (i. e. building up) of the *Body* of Christ." And
this is to be continued "till we all meet in the unity of faith
and of the knowledge of the Son of God, unto a perfect man
unto the measure of the age of the fulness of Christ," in order
that we may not be "children tossed to and fro, and carried
about by every wind of doctrine, in the wickedness
of men, in craftiness by which they lie in wait to decieve." [1].

From these descriptions and definitions of St. Paul we
may turn to the deeds of Jesus Christ the Head of the
Church.

After He had gathered about Him a certain number
of disciples He chose from among them twelve, whom He
sent forth by two and two to preach the Kingdom of God
and heal the sick. "Go not, said the Master, into the way of
the Gentiles, and into the cities of the Samaritans enter
not; but go rather to the lost sheep of the house of Israel." [2]
Later . other seventy are appointed, and "He sent
them two and two before His face into every city and
place whither He Himself was to come." [3]. Of the twelve,
Simon who is called Peter, was chosen to be the Rock on
which the Church was to be built; to him exclusively was
given the Keys of the Kingdom of Heaven ; he received

---

1 Eph. iv, 11-11. 2 Matt. x, 5. 3 Luke x, 1.

separately and in its *plenitude* that power of binding and loosing which subsequently was given to the twelve *collectively ;* [1]
he was selected specially to be the Confirmer of the faith of
all his brethren ; [2] and to him alone was given the fulness
of authority to feed the lambs and the sheep—the whole Flock
of Christ. Thus was the unalterable Constitution of the
Church formed. All teaching power was in Jesus Christ,
the Head, who imparted it to the Apostolic College, reserving special offices to Peter, the Visible Head.

It is well to bear in mind the distinction of meaning in the
word 'Head' as applied to Christ, and as applied to Peter.
From the invisible Head Christ, does the Mystical Body
receive its spiritual life, imparting feeling and motion to the
members. Peter is constituted by Christ visible Head to be
the spring, origin and source of external communion and
government in the Visible Church. So that "IN him," as St.
Augustine has it, "being one, He forms the Church—*in quo
uno (Petro) format Ecclesiam;*" to which St. Jerome's words
may be added: " For this reason out of the twelve one
is selected, that by the appointment of a Head, the occasion
of schism may be taken away."

To these teachers did Jesus before ascending to heaven make
known the whole of that doctrine which He had received of
His Father, and in doing this He completed and closed the
Revelation made to man. He made the Apostles participators in His power of signs and wonders ; cooperators

1 Matt. xvi 18. 19. 2 Luke xxvii, 31.

with Him in pardoning sin by baptism and the sacrament of reconciliation ; to them He imparted the power to consecrate : "Do this in commemoration of me." And as the Father had sent Him so did He send them to preach His Gospel.

This 'Ecclesia docens' or Teaching Body was thus fitted with divine powers for the Ministry of the Gospel, and was duly commissioned by divine authority to 'go and teach ali nations, baptizing them in the name of the Father, and of the Son, and of the Holy Ghost.'

Yet these teachers were commanded by Jesus at the moment of His Ascension that "they should not depart from Jerusalem, but should wait for the promise of the Father which you have heard, said He, by my mouth." And He continued : " It is not for you to know the times or moments which the Father hath put in His own power ; but you shall receive the power of the Holy Ghost coming upon you, and you shall be witnesses unto me in Jerusalem and Samaria and even to the uttermost part of the earth.".[1]

The promise herein referred to was made at the last supper in these words : "And I will ask the Father and He shall give you another Paraclete (Comforter) that he *may abide with you forever ;* the Spirit of Truth, whom the world cannot receive, because it seeeth him not nor knoweth Him ; but you shall know Him, because He shall abide with you, and shall be in you. * * * * * The Paraclete (the

---

1 Acts i, 7, .

Comforter), the Holy Ghost, whom the Father will send in
my name, He will *teach you all things*, and *bring all things*
to your mind whatsoever I shall have said to you * * *
* * When the Paraclete (the Comforter) shall come whom
I will send you from the Father, He *shall give testimony of
me.* * * * * It is expedient for you that I go ; for if
I go not the Paraclete will not come to you ; but if I go I
will send Him to you. And when He shall come, He will
convince the world of sin, and of justice, and of judgment.
* * * * * When He, the Spirit of Truth, shall come
He will *teach you all truth*, for *He shall not speak of Himself*,
but what things soever He shall hear, He shall speak ; and
the things that are to come He will shew you." [1].

It is plain the promise refers to a *new* office which would
be superadded to that which the Holy Ghost already holds.
He was the inspirer of Prophets. He is the Sanctifier of
Men. But the promise declares him to be from that time
and forever the Vivifier of the Body of Christ.

The promise thus made was fulfilled ten days after the
Ascension : "Suddenly there came a sound from heaven as
of a mighty wind coming and it filled the whole house where
they were sitting. And there appeared to them cloven
tongues as it were of fire ; and it sat upon each of them,
and they were all filled with the Holy Ghost, and they be-
gan to speak with divers tongues according as the Holy
Ghost gave them to speak." [2].

---

1 John xiv, 16-26; xvi, 7 and 13. 2 Acts ii, 2-4.

So was born the Church of the living God: Pentecost day
is her birthday. Her organization was conceived and fashioned by *divine* wisdom; She receives a *divine* life; She has
to fulfill a *divine* mission; She is possessed of *divine* power;
She is the appointed guardian of the *divine* revelation. From
that moment and henceforth to the consummation of ages is
this Human-divine Society to have a continuous life in this
world. No power of earth or of hell can destroy it, for
Jesus is its invisible Head, the Holy Spirit its invisible and
active principle of life, and God's power is pledged that
"against it the gates of hell shall not prevail."

Indestructible because of the divine element within, yet
composed of human beings without, it bears outwardly the
manifestation of man's weakness. Hence is the Kingdom of
Heaven likened to ten Virgins, five of whom were foolish ;
to a Net wherein are the clean and the unclean ; to a Marriage feast at which all have not on a marriage garment. In
other words in the outward visible body of the Church the
good and the bad will ever be commingled till the harvest
come. But this destroys not her divine life no more than
sickly or delicate flesh destroys the life of the human being.
In the language of Origen we affirm that ' the Sacred Scriptures assert the whole Church of God to be the Body of
Christ, endowed with life by the Son of God. Of this Body,
which is to be regarded as a whole, the members are individual believers. For as the soul gives life and motion to the
body, which of itself could have no living motion, so the
Word giving a right motion and energy moves the whole

Body, the Church, and each one of its members." [1].

On Pentecost night this Visible Human-divine Society having perfect organization was commensurate with Christianity. None other save itself had the doctrine of Christ ; it alone was the duly appointed Organ for teaching Revelation to men and for dispensing the Mysteries of God. Or as Klee well puts it, "the Church considered internally —*natura naturans*—is Christianity. Christianity considered externally—*natura naturata*—is the Church. The Church and Christianity are Christ in us, and we in Christ. The creature is therefore a Mystical Body, animated by the Spirit of Christ." [2] This is the Kingdom of Christ, the City seated on a Mountain, the Pillar and Ground of Truth, the Temple and Church of the living God, the Bride of the Lamb.

The law of her growth is fixed by God, it is by incorporation, not by accretion. Of the food taken by the human body, are blood, bone and tissue made ; these by assimilation expand or augment the already existing members. So the Mystic Body of Christ absorbs by holy baptism the souls of men receiving them by ones or in numbers. But these additions increase without altering the organization ; they are assimilated to the Body of the Church. Thus is preserved the *identity* of her being, although the individuals composing the visible body are ever varying by death and by spiritual birth. As truly as man, notwithstanding the varying change of the particles of his body, is able to say Ego of every day of life,

---

1 Origen c Celsum VI., 48. 2 Klee, Hist. Christ. Dog. C. on Church.

so too can the Church, the Spouse of Christ speak of her unchanging quasi-personality.

With the growth of her disciples, there was necessarily a growth of her ministers, the *ecclesia docens ;* but here again it is by a fixed law. "How then shall they call on him in whom they have not believed? Or how shall they believe Him of whom they have not heard? And how shall they hear without a preacher? And how can they preach unless they be sent."[1] As the Father sent the Son to preach the Gospel, so did the Son send the Apostles ; they in turn sent others, bishops and priests and deacons, commissioned with the same divine authority to preach and fulfill the Ministry. Accordingly St. John speaking of himself and other pastors could say: "We are of God; he that knoweth God heareth us, he that is not of God heareth not us: in this we know the Spirit of truth and the Spirit of error."[2] And St. Paul in like manner says: "We are ambassadors for Christ, God as it were exhorting by us."[3] To the chief pastors at Ephesus does St. Paul address these words: "Take heed to yourselves, and to the whole flock wherein the Holy Ghost hath placed you bishops, to rule the Church of God."[4] And the Apostles acting in their corporate capacity could proclaim their decree in the name of themselves and of the Holy Ghost.

Knowing that they were possessed of this divine authority in virtue of which Christ had said: " He that heareth you

1, Romans X., 11. 2, 1 John IV., 6. 3, 2 Cor. V., 19. 4, Acts XX., 28.

heareth me; he that despiseth you despiseth me;" the pastors were able to speak as men having power and to exact subjection to their teaching and government in things spiritual. Their Master's words were in their minds: "Whosoever shall not hear you or receive your words when you depart out of that City, shake off the dust from your feet; verily, I say unto you it shall be more tolerable for the land of Sodom and Gomorrah in the day of judgment than for that city." Hence could St. Paul say: "Remember your Prelates who have spoken the word of God to you, whose faith follow,"[1] and again: "Obey your Prelates and be subject to them, for they watch as being to render an account of your souls."[1]

It will be remarked that in appointing these pastors there was (1) 'imposition of hands;' and (2) ' the being sent.'[2] For instance, when the seven deacons were chosen they "were placed in the presence of the apostles, and they praying imposed hands on them."[3] Appointed at first stewards of the Church and distributors of her goods, a part of their office was attendance on the Priests at the divine offices. Later, as we learn, of the seven Stephen was sent to preach; and Philip both preached and baptised.

The ' imposition of hands,' is the sacrament of Orders, and in common with the other sacraments, its effect is conferred direct by God. For this reason, could St. Paul write to Timothy: "I admonish thee that thou stir up the grace of

---

1, Heb. XIII, 7 and 17 2, Acts XIII. 3, Acts VI., 6.

God which is in thee by the imposition of hands." But the
" Commission " or "being sent" is derived direct from the
Apostles. It specifies where, how, and when the divine
authority is to be exercised by the individual pastor. " For
this cause," writes St. Paul to Titus, " I left thee at Crete,
that thou shouldst set in order the things that are wanting,
and shouldst ordain priests in every city, as I also appointed
thee." [1] These two powers are distinguished as the power
of Order, the power of Jurisdiction. Both are of God: the
one comes direct through the sacrament of Orders ; the
other indirectly from God through the Church by Appointment. In the early church they were often conferred
simultaneously ; still they were looked upon as distinct
operations. The power of Jurisdiction is not necessarily
attached to Orders; though for some acts, such as absolution
from sin, both are necessary. The Apostles and the Seventy, who were sent out at first two and two, had jurisdiction
but not orders. A man may be a bishop and yet not be a
bishop of a diocese. On the other hand, a duly and canonically confirmed Bishop Elect possesses jurisdiction without
the Episcopal power to confirm and to ordain ; a deposed
bishop is still possessed of his Episcopal power derived from
consecration, but he is deprived of jurisdiction or cure of
souls. His ordinations would be valid ; his absolutions null
an d void. And thus it would be possible for an organized
bod y of Christians to have valid orders, to hold almost all

---

1. Titus 1, 5.

Catholic doctrines, to offer the great Sacrifice of the Christian Dispensation, and yet be no part of the Church. This was, as a matter of fact, the position of the Novatians and Donatists against whom S. Cyprian and S. Augustin struggled.

The power of Order gives capacity; the power of Jurisdiction permits the use of authority. The distinction between 'can' and 'may,' the former expressing *inherent*, the latter *dependent* power—affords a good illustration of the subject. The dispenser of the power of order is but an instrument ; the grantor of the power of jurisdiction exercises authority and dominion. The first coming directly from Christ is abiding and unchangeable. It is conferred in equal measure on each priest or bishop. The second not coming immediately but through the Church from Christ to individuals, is conferred in varying proportions as may be deemed expedient for the good of souls.

In the instances mentioned above, Timothy and Titus had neither more nor less of Episcopal character than had any of the Apostles : as bishops they were equal. But the Apostles had universal jurisdiction directly from Christ. Timothy and Titus received their commission from the Apostles ; it was restricted to the Church at Ephesus, and to the Church in Crete ; it was neither sovereign nor independent.

Timothy and Titus were consecrated bishops, but the Episcopate of Authority, of which they were appointed participators was one, indivisible, sovereign, and independent.

It was given first in its fulness to Peter *separately ;* later the power of binding and loosing was given *collectively* to the Apostolic College. Thus was granted to the Head 'fulness of supreme power, ordinary and immediate, over all and each of the pastors and of the faithful' in the whole Church, while 'immediate and ordinary jurisdiction' appertains to each bishop in his diocese, but in union and subordination to the Head.

St. Thomas Aquinas, the Prince of Theologians, who died in 1274, that is two centuries previous to the so-called Reformation, expresses with much precision the distinction between Order and Jurisdiction. " Spiritual power," says he, "is twofold : one sacramental, the other jurisdictional. That is sacramental which is bestowed by any consecration ; but all consecrations of the Church are permanent so long as the matter remains which is consecrated, and therefore such power continues in its essence in a man who has received it by consecration as long as he lives, whether he fall into schism or heresy. .... But jurisdictional power is that which is conferred by the concession of man, and therefore such power does not inhere permanently." [1]

By the existence of the one Episcopate is secured, the living cohesion of the Church consisting : " first, of its *unicity* by which there is not, and cannot be a plurality of Christian or co-ordinate churches. Secondly, of its *oneness,* according to which the Church in all its members and parts forms one

1. 2, 2, Q 39, n 3.

entire connected whole."[1] It is not a large crystal, con-
structed of smaller-crystals, but a living organism. The
parable of the Mustard Seed and the metaphor of the Vine
admirably illustrate the point. "I am the vine, you the
branches: he that abideth in Me, and I in him, beareth much
fruit; for without Me you can do nothing. If anyone re-
maineth not in Me, he shall be cast forth as a branch and
shall wither.'

These principles show how utterly untenable is the Branch
Theory of the High Church Party. The Body is *one;* the
Episcopate is *one;* Christianity in its very essence is *one;*
therefore all the branches must be in one and the same
trunk, drawing one and the same divine sap of truth and
authority from one and the same root.

It is not amiss to be reminded when speaking of the "Greek
branch" that it is not one but many. The Russian, the
Hellenic, the Austro-Carlowitzan, the Cypriot, the Monte-
Negran, are so many independent National Churches. On
the other hand, Armenians, Copts, Abyssinians, Nestorians
and Photians are parted by doctrinal or liturgical differ-
ences and antipathies which seem incurable.

While Anglicans have been laboring for Corporate Re-
union, the Greeks have been steadily disintegrating and
forming national religious corporations. In this they have
but followed the way of all Schismatics and Heretics.

Klee on the Church, p. 6.

The authority to be Teachers in the Body of Christ, implies proclaiming the Gospel taught by Christ. He said of Himself that He came to teach not His own doctrine but the doctrine of Him that sent Him. And again, whatever the Father had made known to Him did he communicate to the Apostles. The Spirit of God was to bring to their minds all things whatsoever He had taught them.

These doctrines, and these alone were they to teach; even were "an angel from heaven" to bring any other he was to be anathematized. As there is but One Lord, and one baptism, so is there but one faith says St. Paul. And writing to the Romans [1] "Now I beseech you brethren to mark them who make dissensions and offences contrary to the doctrines which you have learned, and to avoid them."

St. Jude writes his Epistle "to beseech the faithful to contend for the faith once delivered to the Saints," and in the strongest language condemns the wickedness of those who corrupt this true faith by false doctrine. And St. Paul is able to say: "We have received not the spirit of this world, but the spirit of God: that we may know the things that are given us from God: which things also we speak not in the leavened words of human wisdom, but in the doctrine of the spirit, comparing spiritual things with spiritual." [2]

Indeed, this is the very *raison d'etre* of the Church: to dispense the mysteries of God; to conserve in all its purity the deposit of faith ; to proclaim it with divine and therefore infallible or unerring authority to

1, Rom. xvi., 17.   2, Cor. ii., 12

all the sons of men. She is the sole divine inter-
preter and judge of the body of revelation. Hence
when considerable discussions arose at Antioch between
the Jewish and Gentile converts concerning the obligation
of being circumcised according to the law of Moses, it was
determined that Paul and Barnabas and certain others of
the other side should go up to Jerusalem. And on their
arrival "the Apostles and ancients came together to consider of this matter." The question was fully discussed,
and finally the decree was drawn in these words: "it hath
seemed good TO THE HOLY GHOST AND TO US to lay no
further burden on you than these necessary things: that
you abstain from things sacrificed to idols, and from blood,
and from things strangled, and from fornication: from
which things keeping yourselves you shall do well. Fare
ye well." [1] The decree was then sent to the brethren of
the Gentiles that are at Antioch, and in Syria and Cilicia by
the hands of Judas and Silas chief men among the brethren
who accompanied Barnabas and Paul. These who had been
sent received *jurisdiction* to announce by word of mouth the
same things.

In making this decision there was made no addition to
the Faith; the true interpretation of the Revelation already
given was alone proclaimed; and this not by the wisdom of
the Apostles, but by the influence of the Holy Ghost Whom
they declared to be with them. And so has it ever been:

---

(1) Acts xv., 28.

the decisions concerning the Divine personality of Jesus Christ, the procession of the Holy Spirit, the two natures of the Son of God, are not revelations nor additions to the Christian Religion: they are but explicit declarations of what that Faith contains; they do but disclose in detail the Truths of Revelation. These are only the unfoldings of that Faith delivered in its completeness to the Church by Christ.

It will be remarked that Judas and Silas were to confirm *by word of mouth* the decision. This was at first the way in which Christianity was propagated. The Church sent forth her ministers who preached the faith. She therefore had an existence antecedent to the written Gospels; she had numbers of children who lived and believed before a word of the New Testament was written. Her authoritative voice decided when it did come whether it was inspired, and her living teaching and decisions constituted its true interpretation. Six years elapsed before the earliest Gospel, that of St. Matthew, was written; and some sixty-three years had passed by, when the Gospel of St. John made its appearance; and four centuries had elapsed before the Canon of Scripture was settled by Holy Church. Her teaching was *viva voce;* and the inspired books of the New Testament were addressed to those who were already Christians and who had received "the faith once delivered to the Saints." In other words the Christian religion was propagated by LIVING TRADITION.

Scarcely was the Church born, before there were

found those who rebelled against her authority and her doctrine. Such revolt in either case severed individuals from the communion of the Church. They took with them fragments of Christian teaching. Their revolt was considered the greatest of crimes. It is numbered among the sins which exclude from the Kingdom of Heaven. Perhaps no stronger condemnations can be found in the New Testament and the very earliest Christian writers, than those directed against *schism* which is rebellion against the authority of the Church and *heresy* which destroys the oneness of faith. "A man that is a heretic, after the first and second admonition avoid : knowing that he that is such an one is subverted and sineth, being condemned by his own judgment." [1] So does St. Paul instruct Titus. The same Apostle writing to the Galatians [2] groups these crimes with 'murders, fornication,' and other works of the flesh. And the tender Apostle of love, St. John says : " For many seducers are gone out into the world, who confess not that Jesus Christ is come in the flesh; this is a seducer and an anti-Christ. Look to yourselves that you lose not the things which you have wrought ; but that you may receive a full reward. Whosoever receiveth and continueth not in the doctrine of Christ hath not God ; he that continueth in the doctrine, he hath both the Father and the Son. If any man come to you and bring not this doctrine, receive him not into the house nor say to him God speed you. For he

---

1 Titus iii., 10. 2 Gal. v., 19.

that saith to him God speed you communicateth with his wicked works"[1]

St. Clement, whose name St. Paul says is written in the book of life writes to the Corinthians : "Wherefore are there contentions, and swellings, and dissensions, and schisms and war among you ? Have we not one God and one Christ, and one Spirit of Grace poured out upon us, and one calling in Christ ? Wherefore do we rend and tear in pieces the members of Christ and raise a sedition against our own body, and come to such a height of folly as to forget that we are members one of another ?"[2]

St. Irenæus, disciple of St. Polycarp, whose master was the Apostle St. John, writes : "He will also judge those who cause schisms—men destitute of the love of God, and who have in view their own interest, but not the oneness of the Church ; and who, on account of slight and exaggerated causes, rend and divide, and, as far as in them lies, destroy the great and glorious Body of Christ ; men who have peace on their lips but war in their actions ; who truly strain at a gnat but swallow a camel. But no correction can be effected by them so great as is the perniciousness of schism."[3]

The same Apostolic Father says : "The Church, though spread over the whole world, to the earth's boundaries, having received, both from the Apostles and their disciples, the faith in one God, the Father Almighty * * * and in

1, 2, John vii. 2, The citations from the early Christian writers are throughout taken from "The Faith of Catholics." 3 Adv. Hœr. Bk. iv. c. 33.

one Christ Jesus, that Son of God, who was made flesh for
our salvation, and in the Holy Spirit * * * having, as
I have said, received that preaching and this Faith, the
Church, though spread over the whole world guards (it)
sedulously, as though dwelling in one house ; and these
truths she uniformly holds as having but one soul, and one
and the same heart ; and these she proclaims and teaches,
and hands down uniformly, as though she had but one
mouth. For though throughout the world the languages
are various, still the force of the tradition is one and the
same. And neither do the Churches founded in Germany,
nor those of Spain, in Gaul, in the East, in Egypt, in Africa,
nor in the regions in the middle of the earth, believe or deliver a different faith ; but as God's handiwork, the sun, is
one and the same throughout the universe, so the preaching of the truth shines everywhere, and enlightens all men
that wish to come to the knowledge of the truth. Nor does
he, who amongst the rulers in the Churches is more powerful in word, deliver a different doctrine from the above (for
no one is above his teacher) nor does he who is weak in
speech weaken the tradition. For the Faith being one and
the same, neither he who has ability to say much concerning
it hath anything over, nor he that speaketh little anything
lack." [1]

St. Cyprian, A.D. 251, writes in his treatise on the Unity of
the Church :—" The Enemy has made heresies and schisms

---

1 Serm. John xvii, 20.

wherewith to subvert faith, to corrupt truth, and rend unity. Those whom he cannot detain in the blindness of the old way he compasses and deceives by misleading them on their new journey. He snatches men from out of the Church itself.   *   *   *   *

" He who holds not this unity of the Church, does he think that he holds the faith ? He who strives against and resists the Church, he who abandons the Chair of Peter, upon whom the Church was founded, does he feel confident that he is in the Church ?

*   *   *   *

" He is an alien, he is an outcast, he is an enemy. He can no longer have God for a Father who has not the Church for a Mother." " If any one was able to escape who was without the ark of Noah, then can he escape who is out of the doors beyond the Church.

*   *   *   *

" There is one God and one Christ, and His Church is one, and the faith one, and a people one, joined into a solid oneness of body by a cementing concord. Unity cannot be sundered, nor can one body be divided by the dissolution of its structure, nor be cast piecemeal abroad with vitals torn and lacerated. Whatever is parted from the womb cannot live and breathe in its separated state; it loses its principle of life."

Such then is the nature, the constitution, the principle of life, and the law of growth of that Body of Christ divinely appointed to be the Sole Guardian and Teacher of the

Christian Revelation. A living Divine Organism whose unity is to be the criterion of the mission of Jesus, and a visible mark whereby his disciples might be known ; "And not for them only, do I pray, but for them also who *through their word* shall believe in me ; that they all may be one, as thou Father in me and I in thee : that they also may be one in us ; that the *world may believe* that thou hast sent me. And the glory which thou hast given me, I have given to them ; that *they may be one*, as we also are one." [1].

Fashioned during our Lord's Public Life, as to its external organization; born, with its divine internal principle of life, on Pentecost day, the Church is ever to live, sitting in the midst of the nations, day by day instructing and training souls in the way of salvation. Thus is her Life to be *indefectible*, her Voice *infallible*, and her Presence *visible*.

In glowing terms does the late Archbishop Spalding state what her life has been, during the past eighteen centuries and a half. "The Church has triumphantly stood the test of Gamaliel.[*] Empires have arisen, flourished for a time, and then crumbled into ruin, along her pathway in history. Dynasties have changed and been extinguished; thrones have tottered and fallen ; sceptres have been broken; crowns have mouldered into dust; but she has survived all; and she still stands up erect and

---

1, John xvii., 20 and xiii., 35.

[*] Opposing the persecution raised by the Jews he said of the Christian Church : " If this work or design be of men, it will fall to nothing ; but if it be of God, you are not able to destroy it, lest, perhaps, you are found to oppose God." Acts v., 38.

vigorous in the world, not an antique, but a living and breathing existence, having a vitality not sickly, not waning but superabundant ; not only living herself, but bountifully bestowing of her exuberant life upon the nations of the earth, and giving without losing any of it herself; even as the sun giveth forth his light and heat, without impairing his own exhaustless store. She lives, and she will live, all days even to the consummation of the world. She lives, the only divine and immortal institution of the earth. Christ is Head, and Christ is God, and He stands pledged that she shall share in his own immortality. Christ is Her Bridegroom, and she is His chosen Bride, without spot, without wrinkle, all glorious and undefiled; a divine and blooming Bride, who knows no old age and feels no decay, doomed to death, but fated not to die. She has walked the world patiently and longingly, bearing her crown of thorns like her heavenly Bridegroom ; She has been often scourged through it as He was; but like Him, She bears a charmed life ; and cannot be conquered by death. Immortality is written upon her brow, and She will wear the Wreath for ever more, in spite of the world, the devil, and the flesh ! A pilgrim of faith and love with her home in the heavens. She asks only a free passage through this world ; and her Omnipotent Bridegroom will see that She obtain it, whether men will it or not." [1]

---

1 Introduction to Darras's General History of the Church.

II.

The Redemption is limited to no one people. The Precious Blood was shed for all the sons of men. And through its infinite merit every man receives grace sufficient to work out his salvation. To Jesus our Redeemer was given the nations as an inheritance. " Thou art my son," says the inspired Royal Prophet, " Ask of me and I will give thee the Gentiles for thy inheritance, and the uttermost parts of the earth for thy possession." And Isaias announces: "A child is born to us. * * * He shall be called Wonderful, God the Mighty. His empire shall be multiplied. He shall sit upon the throne of David to establish it and strengthen it with judgment and with justice, from henceforth and for ever." [1] The prophet Daniel says : " In the days of those Kingdoms, the God of heaven will set up a Kingdom that shall never be destroyed and His Kingdom shall not be delivered up to another people : and it shall break in pieces and shall consume all these Kingdoms, and itself shall stand for ever." [2] And the Evangelical Prophet declares, " And in the last days the mountain of the House of the Lord shall be prepared on the top of mountains, and it shall be exalted above the hills, and all nations shall flow into it." [3] And Micheas says : "And it shall come to pass in the last days that the mountain of the house of the Lord shall be prepared on the top of mountains and high above the hills, and people shall flow to it. And many nations shall come in haste and say : Come, let us go

---

1 Isaias ix., 6, 7. 2 Dan. ii., 35-44. 3 Isaias ii., 2.

up to the mountain of the Lord and to the House of the
God of Jacob." [1] And the last of the Prophets foretells;
" From the rising of the Sun even to the going down, my
name is great among the Gentiles, and in every place there
is sacrifice, and there is offered to my name a clean obla-
tion, for my name is great among the Gentiles saith the
Lord of Hosts." [2]

So spoke the language of prophecy in clearer and clearer
notes as the time approached for the coming of the Saviour.
His own presence is announced in almost the same words by
the Angel Gabriel: "Thou shalt call his name Jesus. He
shall be great, and shall be called the Son of the Most High,
and the Lord God shall give unto him the Throne of David
his father, and He shall reign in the house of Jacob for ever,
and of his Kingdom there shall be no end." [3]

And as Lactantius wrote fourteen centuries ago : " From
all this it is manifest, that all the prophets foretold of Christ,
that the time would come that being born in the flesh of
the family of David, he would build up to God an everlasting temple called the Church, and would summon all nations to the true religion of God. This is the faithful
house, this the immortal temple, wherein if a man sacrifice
not, he shall not have the reward of immortality. Of which
great and everlasting temple, since Christ was the builder,
the same must needs have therein an everlasting priesthood ; nor can any one come, except through Him who

_____

(1) Mich. xiv., 1. 2. Mal. i., 11, 3 Luke i, 31-33.

built the temple, to the entrance of the temple and to the sight of God."[1]

After having spent three and a half years in laying the foundations of the Kingdom, Jesus sent those whom he had selected and appointed to extend and rule it. " All power is given to me in Heaven and in earth. Going therefore teach ye *all nations*, baptizing them in the name of the Father, and of the Son, and of the Holy Ghost ; teaching them to observe *all things* whatsoever I have commanded you, and behold I am with you *all days* even to the consummation of the world." [2] Thus was it they were to "go into the *whole world* and preach the gospel to *every creature*." [3] And as our Lord said to them : " You shall be witnesses unto me in Jerusalem, and in all Judea, and Samaria, and even to the *uttermost parts* of the earth." [4]

These Scripture statements bear ample evidence that the Church, the Kingdom of Christ, is to be (1) universal in time or duration, (2) universal in extension, (3) universal in doctrine. These constitute the Catholicity of the Church.

The Universality in time flows from the *identity* of life of the quasi-personality of the Church from the moment of birth onwards throughout time. So that of necessity, it can only appertain to the Human-Divine Creature that was born on Pentecost-day to which perpetual duration is promised.

The Universality in extension is the consequence of the Church's *mission* to teach all nations. That for which she has to labor to the end of time, is to bring all men to the light of truth. And were this accomplished she would have

---

1 Divin. Inst., lib. iv., c. 14.   2 Matt. xxviii.,,18-20.   3 Mark xvi. 1, 5.   4 Acts i, 8.

an actual total and absolute physical universality. But she needs time for growth, and unceasing labor to effect conversion and thus extend over the whole world, while conserving her living union in all her parts and organs. On Pentecost evening she was Catholic, though probably she numbered only some three thousand five hundred souls. They were all converts from Judaism, but they joined not a national movement, they had become members of an organization which, *in posse*, though not *in esse* was world-wide.

The Universality in doctrine follows from the Church being the *depository and guardian* of the whole of that Gospel or Deposit of Faith which was in Jesus Christ, and which He committed exclusively to the Human-Divine Creature born on Pentecost day, "to be preserved throughout the ages in its unity and integrity, in its completeness and its purity." [1]

The members of the Church received a name for the first time at Antioch, where, the Scripture narrates, they were called "Christian." This may have been done in derision by the Jews or Romans, or it may have been the name chosen by the Disciples themselves. The outer world called the children of the Church Nazarenes, Galilæans, Jesseans, Therapeutæ ; and in the writings of the first Fathers are they spoken of as the Believers, the Saints, the Elect. But of all their titles that of *Catholic* was applied to them from the earliest period, and has remained to them as an exclusive and inalienable name.

---

1 Humphrey "Other Gospels," p. 62.

Long before the formal symbol of the Councils of Nice and Constantinople—"I believe in the One-Holy Catholic and Apostolic Church"—had the name Catholic been used.

Before the Apostles died, their sound had gone forth to the furthermost parts of the earth, and the Church had extended far and wide throughout the Roman Empire from the very household of Cæsar wherein the bonds of St. Paul were manifest in all the palace.[1] And Tertullian, whose death is put at the latest A. D. 240 is able to write: "Men cry out that the State is beset, that the Christians are in their fields, in their forts, in their islands. They mourn, as for a loss, that every sex, age, condition, and now even rank, is gone over to this sect." [2]

It is not surprising, therefore, that the name *Catholic* should, of all others, have been applied to them, and that they themselves should have embeded it in their Creeds. Those without saw the Christian Body made up of all nations and of all grades of men. Those within knew they were members of a kingdom which is to be world-wide, and never ending on earth ; they felt themselves possessors of a religion designed for the whole man and for the entire human race. So Catholic Church was synonimous with the Christian people; and the Catholic Faith meant the true or orthodox gospel.

The word appears for the first time, so far as can be ascertained, in a passage of a letter of St. Ignatius,

---

1 Phil. iv., 22 and i, 13.   2 Apol. n. i, p. 2.

a disciple of the Evangelist, St. John, and second successor of the Apostle, St. Peter in the See of Antioch. "Where the bishop is, there let the multitude of believers be; even where Jesus Christ is, there is the Catholic Church." And this same writer, in the Introduction to the Martyrdom of St. Polycarp, writes: "The Church of God which dwelleth in Smyrna, to the Church of God which dwelleth in Philomelium and all the districts in every place of the Holy and Catholic Church mercy, peace and love from God the Father and our Lord Jesus Christ." In the body of the piece occurs twice the same phrase: "After he had done praying having made mention of all with whom he had ever met, great and small, noble and obscure, and after the whole Catholic Church throughout the world" (n. 8). "He Christ is both the Governor of our bodies and the Shepherd of the Catholic Church throughout the world (n. 19). This document is written about A. D. 147." [1]

St. Irenæus, who was born about 140 in Asia Minor, became bishop of Lyons in 178, and was martyred in 202, he writes in his work against Heresies: "When they believed not, last of all he sent his Son, our Lord Jesus Christ, whom, when the wicked husbandmen had slain, they cast him out of the vineyard. Wherefore did the Lord God deliver it, now no longer fenced in, but opened unto *the whole world*, to other husbandmen, who give in the fruits in their season;

---

1 Faith of Catholics, Vol. I. p. 288; other extracts from same.

the tower of election being *everywhere* exalted and beautiful.
For *everywhere* is the Church distinctly visible, and *everywhere* is there a wine press dug ; for *everywhere* are those
who receive the Spirit." [1]

" In the acts of the Martyrs, Baronius gives the following
most interesting interrogatory of the year 254. " Polemon
the judge interrogates the martyrs. What is your name?
Pisonius, says ; Christian. Of what Church ? Pisonius,
replies: of the Catholic....What are you called? She
answered : Theodora and a Christian. Polemon: if she is
Christian of what Church. But she responds: of the
Catholic."

S. Cyril of Jerusalem in his Catechetical Discourses, delivered in the year 347, says : "When you go to any city do
not ask merely for the House of God or for the Church
merely for all heretics pretend to have this : but ask which
is the Catholic Church, for this title belongs to our Holy
Mother alone.[2]"

And again : "'The faith which we rehearse contains in
order the following : ' And into one baptism of repentance
for the remission of sins, and into one holy Catholic Church.'
. . . . Now it is called Catholic, because it is throughout the whole world, from one end of the earth to the other;
and because it teaches universally (catholically) and completely all the doctrines which ought to come to men's knowledge concerning things both visible and invisible, heavenly
and earthly ; and because it subjugates unto godliness

1 Ibid. 2 Cat. Dis. XVIII, 27.

(or to the true religion) the whole race of men, both governors and governed, learned and unlearned, and because it
universally treats and heals every sort of sins committed by
soul and body, and possesses in itself every form of virtue
which is named, both in deeds and words, and every kind
of spiritual gifts. And it is rightly called Church, because
it calls forth and assembles together all men."

Eusebius, Bishop of Cæserea, the Father of Ecclesiastical History, who lived from about 270 till 340,
writes : "The false accusations invented by our Pagan
enemies quickly disappeared self-refuted, whilst fresh sects
sprang up anew upon sects ; the first always passing away,
and corrupted, in a variety of ways, into other views of
many modes and forms. But the splendor and solemnity
and sincerity and liberty of the Catholic and alone true
church,—a church always holding uniformly to the same
things,—still went on increasing and magnifying."

St. Pacian, Bishop of Barcelona, fifteen centuries
ago wrote a short treatise on the name "Catholic."
Therein does he use these words: "My brother, fret not
yourself; Christian is my name, but Catholic my surname.
That names me, this describes me; by this I am approved;
by that designated. And if at last we must give an
account of the word Catholic, and express it, from the Greek
by a Latin interpretation, "Catholic is everywhere one, or as
the more learned think, obedience in all "—all the commandments of God. . . . Therefore he who is a Catholic, the
same is obedient to what is right. He who is obedient, the

same is a Christian. And thus the Catholic is a Christian.
Wherefore our people, when named Catholic, are separated
by this appellation from the heretical name. But if also the
word Catholic means 'everywhere one' as those first think,
David indicates this very thing when he says : 'The Queen
stood in a gilded clothing, surround with variety, (Ps. xliv,
10), that is one amidst all.' . . . Amidst all, she is one,
and one over all. If thou askst the reason of the name, it is
manifest."

And not to weary with extracts, the following will suffice
from the great St. Augustine, Bishop of Hippo, in Africa,
who died in 430, and who, in common with the other
Fathers cited, belong to what the High Church party call
the "Undivided Church." "In the Catholic Church, not
to mention that most sound wisdom, to the knowledge of
which a few spiritual men attain in this life, so as to know it
in a very small measure, indeed for they are but men, but still
to know it without doubtfulness—for not quickness of understanding, but simplicity in believing, that make the rest of
masses most safe—not to mention therefore this wisdom
which you Manichees do not believe to be in the Catholic
Church, many other reasons there are which most justly keep
me in her bosom. The agreement of peoples and nations
keeps me; an authority begun with miracles, nourished with
hope, increased with charity, strengthened by antiquity, keeps
me; the succession of priests from the chair itself of the Apostle Peter—unto whom the Lord after his resurrection committed His sheep to be fed—down even to the present bishop,
keeps me; finally, the name itself of the Catholic Church

keeps me—a name, which in the midst of so many heresies, this Church alone has not without cause so held possession of, as that, though all heretics would fain have themselves called ' Catholics,' yet to the enquiry of any stranger 'where is the meeting of the Catholic Church held?' no heretic would dare point out his own basilica or house. Those, therefore, so numerous and so powerful ties of the Christian name, ties most dear, justly keep a believing man in the Catholic Church, even though through the slowness of our understanding or the deservings of our lives, truth shew not herself as yet in her clearest light. Whereas, amongst you, where are none of these things to invite and keep me ; there is only the loud promise of truth."

Wondrous delineation of the great Bishop of Hippo; though written fifteen centuries ago, it is as fresh in its truthfulness as if it were but of yesterday. Newman's words do but re-echo the touching words of St. Augustine : "There is one, and only one religion such (i. e. having priests and sacrifices, and mystical rites, and the monastic rule, and care for the souls of the dead, and the profession of an ancient faith, coming through all ages from the Apostles): it is known everywhere; every poor boy in the street knows the name of it; there never was a time, since it first was, that its name was not known, and known to the multitude. It is called *Catholicism*, a world wide name, and incommunicable; attached to us from the first; accorded to us by our enemies; in vain attempted, never stolen from us by our rivals."[1] Both writers must have had in mind the inspired passage of the prophet Isaias: "My spirit that is in thee, and my words that I have put into thy mouth, shall not depart out of thy mouth, nor out of the mouth of thy seed, nor out of the mouth of thy seed's seed, saith the Lord from henceforth and for ever."[2]

III.

Distant as were the British Isles from the seat of the government of Imperial Rome, yet at an early period in the History of the Church was the Gospel proclaimed to their inhabitants.

It is conjectured by some that St. Paul was the first to bring the *glad tidings*. If so, then beyond doubt was the Church in Britain in thorough communion with, and under the authority of the Apostles.

But from conjecture we may pass to history written in the infancy of the Church, a little more than a century after the landing of St. Augustin. Venerable Bede informs us that as early as the second century, a British King, Lucius by name, sent to Pope Eluthcrius, then governing the Church, to ask for instructions in the Christian law. Missionaries were accordingly sent, and the Church was planted in Britain. The same historian tells us that "Palladius was sent by Celestine, the Roman Pontiff, to the Scoti, who believed in Christ, to be their first Bishop." This statement is confirmed by St. Prosper, in his Chronicle; and he further adds

1. Occ. Serm. p. 110. 2 Cap. lix., 21.

that in A. D. 429, when the Christian faith was endangered by the heresy of the Pelagians, the same Pope Celestine, at the request of Palladius, sent as his deputy—" *Vice sua mittit*"—Germanus, Bishop of Auxerre, accompanied by Lupus, bishop of Troyes, into Britain to defend the faith and arrest if possible the growth of the heresy.

Of the success of that mission Venerable Bede gives this testimony : " The triumph of orthodoxy was complete, and Germanus before he quitted the scene of victory visited the tomb of S. Alban, where he deposited a small box of relics that he brought with him from Gaul, taking in exchange a handful of dust from the grave, that he might place it in a new church at Auxerre which he afterwards dedicated in honor of the British martyr." [1]

It is well known that at the Council of Arles, France, held in 314, three British Bishops, York, Lincoln and London were of the assembled fathers, they shared in the deliberations of the Council, took part in the Acta, and signed the Synodal letter addressed to the Pope, wherein it is declared the chief part of the government of the Church devolves according to ancient usage on the Roman Pontiff.

And S. Athanius tells us [2] that at the Council of Sardica, held in 347, in which he himself was so prominent a figure, there were Bishops of Britain who participated in its work. The same Saint tells us its decrees were signed or agreed to by more than 300 Bishops. In its third, fourth and fifth Canons the right of the Pope to receive appeals is dis-

---

1 Beda, i. c. 18. 2 Apol. c. Arian, i. vol. i, p. 123.

tinctly recognized. The Bishops from Britain in common
with the other assembled fathers, addressed Pope Julius in
these words : "It will seem to be best and most proper if
the bishops from each particular province report to the
Head, that is to the See of Peter the Apostle." [1]

These and similar facts bear the clearest evidence that the
Church in Roman Britain received its doctrine from the
Holy See ; that it was subject to the authority of the Pope;
and that it was in full communion with the Universal
Church. It knew no other faith than that defined in the
General Councils of Nice and Constantinople. The Bishops
of Britain and their flocks held the same faith as St.
Athanasius, Bishop of Alexandria, St. Cyril, Bishop of
Jerusalem, St. Ambrose, Bishop of Milan, St. Augustine,
Bishop of Hippo, St. Basil the Great, Bishop of Cœserea,
St. Pacian, Bishop of Barcelona, St. Gregory, Bishop of
Nyssa, St. John Chrysostom, Bishop of Constantinople: all
of whom lived *in the same century* in which we have the his-
toric evidence that the Bishops from Britain took part in the
Councils of Arles, Sardica, and Rimini.

" From *national animosity* the Britains who were Catholic
and had been driven to the western part of the island refused to communicate the doctrines of the Gospel to the
Saxons, and continued as late as a century after the arrival
of Aidan to look upon the Saxon christians, even on those
who had been converted by Scottish missionaries, as no
better than pagans, and treated them on all occasions as

---

1 Ep. Synd. Sard., Hard. Col. con. Vol. I.

aliens from Christianity." * This was but natural, and in no way proves there was difference of faith or of church.

It is sometimes urged the Church in Britain was Greek rather than Latin, and therefore independent of Rome. But objectors should remember that Greeks and Latins were then of one "Undivided Church"; and that Christianity having begun in Asia Minor, it is natural to expect that Greek missionaries and with them Greek customs should be found throughout the infant Church. This instead of militating against the unity of the Church is an argument in its favor. St. Irenæus though born in Asia Minor, comes to Lyons as its Bishop in 178 A. D.

St. Irenæus knew of no "independence of Rome." For he writes that the Roman Church is the chief, the head and first of all; the greatest, the most ancient and most re-nowned; founded by St. Peter, the Prince of the Apostles, and his companion, St. Paul; the Church which by its own *right presides and rules over all the rest, and with which it is necessary that all the faithful should be united by bonds of one and the same faith and communion.†*

It is plain the position of the present Anglican National Church in no way resembles the position of the Church in Britain to the Universal Church. But the very attempt to connect the Church *of* England with the Church *in* Britain is a flagrant violation of historical truth.

It must be remembered the present Anglican Communion

---

* Lingard Hist. Aug. Sax. Church, p. 13. † See the admirable Cathedra Petri by Allnatt, p. 86.

can claim no descent from the British Church. Its paren-
tage, like that of the English nation, is Anglo-Saxon.
For when the barbarous hordes of Angles, Jutes and Saxons in the fifth century invaded Britain, they drove the inhabitants into the western parts of the island, and then
located themselves on the depopulated lands. The Britons
with their Catholicism were driven to the mountainous districts of the West. England was once more a land of
heathens. Its conversion was to be effected a second time.

Again did Rome undertake the arduous work. St. Gregory
the Great sent in 596 St. Augustine to convert the Anglo-
Saxons to the true and living God. The zealous Apostle
found the whole of the Saxon part of the country in a state
of paganism, and the conquered Britons in the West under
the rule of one Archbishop and seven Bishops. In a few
years Christianity made such progress that the Hierarchy
was established with St. Augustine as the first Archbishop
of Canterbury. At the command of St. Gregory the Great,
—" *Juxta quod jussa Sancti Patri Gregorii acceperant*"—
Augustine received *Episcopal consecration* from Virgilius the
Primate of Arles ; but the *Archiepiscopal jurisdiction*, and
mission in the See of Canterbury Augustine received from
Pope Gregory himself. A little later the same Roman Pontiff empowered Augustine to erect two provinces, Canterbury and York, each with its suffragan Bishops. Thus
was the Hierarchy of the Church in England fashioned by
the hand of Pope Gregory the Great, and maintained by
him. What was given in the first instance by Gregory was

granted to each Archbishop of Canterbury by the Roman
Pontiffs, successors of St. Gregory. And so mission and
jurisdiction to govern the whole Church in England proceeded perpetually from St. Peter's Chair.

The isolation of the British Bishops caused by the Saxon
invasion had, as Gildas, a British author of the middle of
the sixth century, informs us, brought about the most de-
plorable results ; hence, in instituting Augustine Archbishop, Pope Gregory the Great writes ; "We commit to
your brotherly care all the Bishops of Britain, that the unlearned may be taught, the weak strengthened by persua-
sion, the perverse corrected by authority." [1] And later the
Pope writes : "We give you no authority over the Bishops
of Gaul, because from the ancient times of my predecessors
the Bishop of Arles received the pallium, whom we must
not deprive of the authority with which he is invested." [2]

By the way, these acts and statements of St. Gregory the
Great throw much light on the sense in which he rejected
the title of "Universal Bishop." He himself tells us because
it appeared to imply the idea that he alone was bishop:
"*Solus conetur appellari Episcopus.*" But this did not prevent him believing and acting on the belief as we here see,
that as Pope he was Bishop of Bishops.

The work begun under Pope Gregory was completed in
little more than half a century later by Theodore the Greek
Monk nominated Archbishop by Pope Vitalian. "We learn
your desire," says Vitalian, "for the *confirmation* of the diocese subject to you because you desire to shine by our

---

1. Bede, i, 27. 2. Ep., lxiv.

privilege of apostolic authority. Wherefore we have thought good at present to *commend to your most wise Holiness all the Churches in the Island of Britain.* But now by authority of Blessed Peter, Prince of the Apostles to whom power was given by our Lord to bind and to loose in Heaven and on earth, we however unworthy holding the place of that same Blessed Peter who bears the keys of the Kingdom of Heaven, grant to you Theodore and your successors, all that from old time was allowed, forever to remain unimpaired in that, your Metropolitan See in the City of Canterbury." [1]

The Church in England thus was duly organized and received the Episcopal and Parochial form which the Anglican Communion retains till this day. So solid were the fruits of Archbishop Theodore's labors that as Stubbs, the distinguished living Protestant historian says: " In a single century England became known to Christendom as a fountain of light, as a land of learned men, of devout and unwearied missions, of strong and pious Kings."[2] And another Protestant historian, Guizot, says: " As to the Anglo-Saxon Church, you know that having been founded by the Popes themselves, it was placed from the commencement under their most direct influence."[3]

Sixty-eight Archbishops succeeded St. Augustine in the See of Canterbury. Each received the pallium—the em-

---

1 Mansi, vol. xi., 24. 2. Const.. Hist., Vol. i, 251. 3. Cours d' Histoire Modern, iii. p. 07.

blem of Metropolitan power—from the Pope of Rome.
" Pope Agatho limited the number of bishops to one Metropolitan and eleven Suffragans. Leo II established a
second Metropolitan at York ; Adrian a third at Lichfield,
and confirmed to the Church of Canterbury that preced-
ence of rank and authority which it has since possessed
down to the present day."[1] From this fountain-head of
jurisdiction, spiritual authority flowed through the hierarchy of the Church to the people of England. In
disputes concerning doctrine or ecclesiastical discipline, the English Kings, Bishops and People had recourse
to the Holy See as the final court of appeal, and to the
Roman Pontiff as the Vicar of Christ and Supreme Judge
on earth in matters ecclesiastical. The famed case of S.
Wilfred, appealing in 676 from his Metropolitan, Theodore,
to the Pope, is known to every student of history.

There were, it is true, at times, conflicts with Rome.
Sundry acts in the Statute Book bear evidence that the
English nation resisted claims made by some of the Popes
to interfere in the civil affairs of the country, to certain
revenues, to the appointment of foreigners to benefices,
and the like. Such claims clearly enough sprang not from
the Divine and essential character of the Papacy, but from
the civil position and rights created by the nations of
Europe, and conferred by them on the Sovereign Pontiff
in the Middle Ages at a time when Feudalism was the

1. Lingard, Ant. of Ang-Sax. Ch. Vol. i, c, 8.

governing spirit, and the Pope was not only held to be the divinely appointed Head of the Church, but also was the unanimously elected Father of the Christian nations. The English people knew well how to separate the Spiritual from the Temporal Authority of the Pope, and, while questioning some of the feudal claims of the latter, rendered dutiful and filial obedience to the former. The English people knew, as Venerable Bede said : "Gregory was invested with the first, that is, *supreme pontificate*, in *the whole world*, and was set over the Churches converted to the true Faith, he made our nation, till then given up to idols, the Church of Christ."[1] And in the prayer of their Anglo-Saxon Pontifical for the consecration of a new Pope, he is described as "This Thy servant whom Thou hast made Prelate of the Apostolic See, and Primate of *all the priests in the world*, and Teacher of Thy Universal Church, and whom Thou hast chosen for the ministry in the High Priesthood."

During the rule of these sixty-nine Archbishops of Canterbury, monasteries were founded in every part of England. Public schools and universities, guilds and charitable institutions were called into existence. Every parish had erected its church, every diocese its cathedral : these still remain living monuments of the generosity and faith of our Catholic Forefathers.

In such Temples of the living God, under the invocation of the Blessed Virgin or some Saint, were the altars on which was offered the propitiatory sacrifice of the Mass for

---

1 Bede Hist., ii, c. I.

the living and for the dead. There was the Tabernacle in which dwelt the Holy of Holies under the sacramental species. From the pulpits of such Temples One same Faith was preached with spiritual and divine authority by those duly commissioned, directly or indirectly, by Rome. The people held living communion with Christendom, and, as is witnessed by the Chantry and Ladye Chapels of the Sacred Edifices, they held practical communion with the Souls in Purgatory and with the Saints in Paradise.

Begotten by Pope Gregory the Great, nurtured and governed by Papal Power, the Church in England covered the whole land and grew for nine hundred and sixty years. Its independence of the State was secured by Magna Charta, in these words : " The English Church is of Divine right, free, and its laws and liberties are not to be violated." Church and State grew side by side in harmony, rendering mutual aid, and formed " Merrie England." So was it until the accession of the Tudors, under whom a mighty and radical change was effected.

With the Wars of the Roses ended in great measure the power of the nobles. Henry VII and his successors determined to hold absolute power. " What the first of the Tudors," says the late distinguished historian, Green, a clergyman of the Church of England, " had done for the political independence of the Kingdom, the second was to do for its ecclesiastical independence. * * * * The last check on Royal absolutism which had survived the Wars of

V

the Roses, lay in the wealth, the independent synods and
jurisdiction and claims of the Church ; and for the success
of the new policy it was necessary to reduce the great ecclesiastical body to a mere *department of the State, in which all
authority should flow from the sovereign alone, his will be the
only law, his decision the only test of truth.*"

Most thoroughly was this accomplished. To attain the
end, separation from Rome, the fountain of Spiritual governing power was absolutely necessary. At the outset the
movement appeared to be but an individual act inspired by
Cromwell ; the divorce of Queen Catherine was but a pre-
text for it ; the real purpose in establishing the Royal Supremacy was to make the sovereign absolute. How this
was effected we shall now see.

In 1533 an Act of Parliament was passed in which it was
declared that the King "is Supreme Head of the Church of
England, as the Prelates and Clergy of your Realm representing the said Church in said Synods and Convocations
have recognized." [1]

And again : The King "is the Supreme Head of the
Church of England, and so is recognized by the Clergy of
this Realm in this Convocation" [2] ; and the Statute declares
that as Head in Earth of the Church of England,
the King has all "pre-eminences, jurisdictions, privileges,
authorities to the said dignity belonging, and especially
full power to repress, correct and amend all *heresies*

---

1 Henry viii., 21. 2 26 Henry viii., 3.

and abuses which by any manner, *spiritual authority or jurisdiction*, ought to be repressed, corrected or amended." And later still was it asserted by Parliament: "Archbishops, Bishops, Archdeacons and other ecclesiastical persons have no manner of jurisdiction ecclesiastical, but by, under and from your Royal Majesty." [1]

These atrocious claims were put forward by the King; and a time-serving Parliament assigned his behests. To the honor of the English people, be it said, they took no part in the matter. Then and throughout they were robbed of their Faith and of the Church, their birthright. The aristocracy had been almost annihilated, and the power of the people had not been developed. The new order of things was thrust upon them, and, as has been well said, "Henry VIII fixed his supremacy on a reluctant Church by the axe, the gibbet, the stake, and laws of premunire and forfeiture." Bishop Burnet, the laudatory historian of the so-called reformation, confessed that all the efforts of the Government to overcome the dislike of the people to Protestantism had been in vain, and that a troop of German mercenaries had to be brought over from Calais in 1549 to conquer their resistance. "With eleven-twelfths of the people," said at that time Paget to the Duke of Somerset the Protector, "the new religion has found no entrance." There were men who would not bend their knee to Baal, and died martyrs because they could not accept Royal Supremacy,

---

[1] 1 37 Henry VIII., 17.

but stood true to the supreme authority of the Pope in
things spiritual. Among them Fisher, Bishop of Rochester,
and Sir Thomas Moŗe, the Chancellor. "This indict-
ment," says the latter in his memorable defence, "is ground-
ed upon an Act of Parliament directly repugnant to the
laws of God and His Holy Church, * * * * and therefore, my Lord, I do not think myself bound to conform my
conscience to the counsel of one Kingdom against the general consent of all christendom."

The Archbishop of Canterbury, in his commendatory letter, introducing the Bishop of Rochester from England to
the last Convention at Philadelphia as the successor of the
first Bishop of Rochester, ought in common honesty, to have
added--but with Bishop Fisher of Rochester beheaded in
1535 under Henry VIII for boldly upholding the faith
and authority of the first Bishop of this See, ended the succession in doctrine and jurisdiction brought from Rome.
The magnificent statement of the case made by this Martyr
Bishop before Convocation so fully expresses the teaching of
his predecessors that it will be well to give the whole
speech.

" My lords," he said, " it is true we are under the king's
lash, and stand in need of the king's good favour and
clemency, yet this argues not that we should therefore do
that which will render us both ridiculous and contemptible
to all the Christian world, and *hissed out from the society of
God's holy Catholic Church;* for what good will that be to
us, to keep the possession of our houses, cloisters, and

convents, and to lose the society of the Chtistian world, to preserve our goods and lose our consciences? Wherefore, my lords, I pray, let us consider what we do, and what it is we are to grant, the dangers and inconveniencies that will ensue thereupon, or whether it lies in our power to grant what the king requests at our hands, or whether the king be an apt person to receive this power, that so we may go groundedly to work, and not like men that had lost all honesty and wit together with their worldly fortune. As concerning the *first* point, viz., what the supremacy of the Church is which we are to give unto the king, it is to exercise the spiritual government of the Church in chief, which, according to all that I have ever learned, both in the Gospel and through the whole course of divinity, mainly consists in these two points; first, in loosing and binding sinners, according to that which our Saviour said unto Peter, when He ordained him head of His Church, viz., *To thee I will give the keys of the kingdom of heaven.* Now, my lords, can we say unto the king, *Tibi*, to thee will I give the Keys of the Kingdom of Heaven? If you say Yes, where is your warrant? If you say No, then you have answered yourselves that you cannot put such Keys into his hands. *Secondly.* The supreme government of the Church consists in feeding Christ's sheep and lambs, according unto that time when our Saviour performed that promise unto Peter, making him His universal shepherd by such unlimited jurisdiction, *feed My lambs*, and not only so, but feed those that are the feeders of those lambs, *feed My sheep.* Now, my lords, can any of us say unto the king *pasce oves?* God hath given unto His Church some to be apostles, some evangelists, some pastors, some doctors, that they might edify the body of Christ; so that you must make the king one of these before you can set him over these, And when you have made him one of these supreme Heads of the Church, he must be such a head as may be answerable to all the members of Christ's body. And it is not the few ministers of an island that must constitute a Head over the universe; or, at least, by such example we must allow as many Heads over the Church as there are sovereign powers within Christ's dominion, and then what will become of the supremacy? Every member must have a head. *Attendite vobis* was not said to kings but to bishops. *Thirdly.* Let us consider the inconveniences that will arise upon this grant. We cannot grant this unto the king but we must renounce our unity with the See of Rome. And if there were no further matter in it than a renouncing of Clement VII. Pope thereof, then the matter were not so great; but in this we do forsake the first *four* General Councils, which none ever forsook; we renounce all canonical and ecclesiastical laws of the Church of Christ, we renounce all other Christian princes, we renounce the unity of the Christian world, and so leap out of Peter's ship to be drowned in the wave of all heresies, sects, schisms, and divisions; for the first and general Council of Nice acknowledged Silvester, the Bishop of Rome, his authority to be over them by sending their decrees to be ratified by him. The Council of Constantinople did acknowledge Pope Damasus to be their chief by admitting him to give sentence against the heretics Macedonius, Sabellius, and Eunomius. The Council of Ephesus acknowledged Pope Celestin to be their chief judge by admitting his condemnation upon the heretic Nestorius. The council of Chalcedon acknowledged Pope Leo to be their chief head, and all general councils of the world ever acknowledged the Pope of Rome only to be the supreme Head of the Church; and now, shall we acknowledge another Head, or one Head to be in England, and another in Rome? *Fourthly.* We deny all canonical and ecclesiastical laws, which wholly do depend upon the authority of the Apostolic See of Rome. *Fifthly.* We renounce the judgment of all other Christian princes, whether they be Protestants or Catholics, Jews or Gentiles, for by this argument Herod must have been Head of the Church of Jews, Nero must have been Head of the Church of Christ, the Emperor must be Head of the Protestant Churches in Germany, and the Church of Christ must never have had a Head till about three hundred years after Christ. *Sixthly.* The King's Majesty is not susceptible of this donation. Ozias, for meddling with the priest's office, was resisted by Azarias, thrust out of the temple, and told that it belonged not to his office. Now, if the priest spake truth in this, then is the king not to meddle in this business; if he spoke amiss why did God plague the king with leprosy for this, and not the priest? King David, when the Ark of God was in bringing home, did he place himself at the head of the priests' order? Did he so much as touch the ark, or execute any the least properly belonging to the priests' function? or rather did he not go before and *abase himself among the people*, and say that he would become yet more vile, so that God might be glorified? All good Christian emperors have evermore refused ecclesiastical authority, for at the first General Council of Nice certain bills were privily brought unto Constantine to be ordered by his authority, but he caused them all to be burned, saying, '*Dominus vos constituit*,' *&c.*—God hath ordained you priests, and hath given you power to be judges over us, and therefore by right in these things we are to be judged by you, but you are not to be judged by us.' Valentine, the good emperor, was required by the bishops to be present with them to reform the heresy of the Arians, but he answered, 'For as much as I am one of the members of the lay people, it is not lawful for me to define such controversies, but let the priests to whom God hath given charge thereof, assemble where they will in due order.' Theodosius, writing to the Council of Ephesus, saith, 'It is not lawful for him that is not of the holy order of bishops to intermeddle with ecclesiastical matters.' And now shall we cause our King to be Head of the Church, which all good kings abhorred the very least thought thereof, and so many wicked kings have been plagued for so doing? Truly, my lords, I think they are his best friends that dissuade him from it, and he would be the worst enemy to himself if he should obtain it. *Lastly*, if this thing be, farewell to all unity with Christendom; for

as that holy and blessed martyr, St. Cyprian, saith, 'All unity
depends upon the authority of that Holy See, as upon the
authority of Peter's successors.' For, saith the same holy
father, all heresies, sects, and schisms have no other use but
this, that men will not be obedient to the chief bishop. And
now for us to shake off our communion with that Church,
either we must grant the Church of Rome to be the Church
of God or else a malignant Church. If you answer she is
of God, and a Church where Christ is truly taught, His
sacraments rightly administered, &c., how can we forsake,
how can we flee from such a Church? Certainly we ought
to be with and not to separate ourselves from such a one.
If we answer that the Church of Rome is not of God, but a
malignant Church, then it will follow that we the inhabitants
of this island have not as yet received the true faith of
Christ. Seeing we have not received any other doctrine,
any other sacraments than what we have received from her,
as most evidently appears by all the ecclesiastical histories,
wherefore, if she be a malignant Church, we have been
deceived all this while. And if to renounce the common
Father of all Christendom, all the general councils, especially
the first four, which none renounce, all the countries of
Christendom, whether they be Catholic or Protestant, be to
forsake the unity of the Christian world, there is the grant-
ing of the *supremacy* of the Church unto the King, a
renouncing of this unity, a tearing of the seamless coat of

Lewis' Life of Fisher Vol. ii., 58.

Christ in sunder, a dividing of the mystical body of Christ, His spouse, limb from limb, and tail to tail, like Samson's foxes, to set the field of Christ's holy Church all on fire. And this is what we are about; wherefore, let it be said to you in time, and not too late, Look you to that."

Would the present Bishop of Rochester, or any of his brothers in the Anglican Episcopate, or any of their predecessors for the past three hundred years, seal with their blood this teaching of the Martyr Bishop Fisher? The Bishops of Rochester during three centuries have repudiated this which was the teaching of the Church *in* England, and in common with the rest of the Bishops of the Establishment have become mere agents of the English Sovereign, bowing down before Royal Supremacy.

Commenting on the Statute 26 Henry VIII, assigning the King the Headship of the Church of England, Coke and Blackstone say that by it "all that power which the Pope ever exercised within the realm in spirituals is now annexed to the Crown." Henry determined it should be so, and exacted an Oath of Supremacy of his subjects, whereby they "from henceforth utterly renounce, refuse, relinquish er forsake the Bishop of Rome his authority," and "shall accept, repute and take the King's Majesty to be the only Supreme Head in Earth of the Church of England."

The boy King, Edward VI, walked in the steps of his father, re-asserted the spiritual claims of his parent, and acted on them. Listen to the words of his Parliament:

"His Highness * * * * hath appointed the Archbishop of Canterbury, and certain of the most learned and discreet Bishops, and other learned men of the realm to * * * * make one convenient and meet, order, rite and fashion of common prayer."[1] Read His Majesty's patent for the appointment of bishops: "We name, make, create, constitute and declare *N* Bishop of *N*, to have and to hold to himself the said bishopric during the term of his natural life, if for so long a time he behave himself well therein; and *empower him to confer order*, to institute to livings, to exercise *all manner of jurisdiction, and to do all that appertains to the episcopal or pastoral office*, over and above the things known to have been committed to him by God in the Scriptures, *in place of us, in our name, and by our authority.*"

The Statutes of Henry and Edward, levelled at Papal jurisdiction, and attributing all ecclesiastical authority to the Crown, though repealed under Mary were at the very outset of Elizabeth's reign re-enacted and enforced in all their vigor. Her Majesty's obsequious Parliament declared in different acts that the spiritual authority of every foreign prelate within the realm should be utterly abolished; that the jurisdiction necessary for the correction of errors, heresies, schisms and abuses should be annexed to the Crown, with the power of delegating such jurisdiction to any person or persons whatever at the pleasure of the Sovereign; that the penalty of asserting the Papal authority should ascend

---

1 Edward VI., 1.

on the repetition of the offence from the forfeiture of real and personal property to perpetual imprisonment, and from perpetual imprisonment to death. And that all clergymen should, under pain of deprivation, take an oath declaring the Queen to be *Supreme Governor in all ecclesiastical and spiritual things in causes*, renouncing all foreign, ecclesiastical, and spiritual jurisdiction or authority whatsoever within the realm."[1] We have thus ample proof that the jurisdiction and authority of the Pope were denied, rejected and repudiated by Acts of Parliament, and that the Civil Power reduced the Church *in* England to be the Church *of* England. Thus was it made a Department of State, deriving its authority and jurisdiction from the Crown, just as do the Army and the Judges.

Ever since that power was asserted to be conferred on Elizabeth in 1558 by the Parliament, every clergyman of the Established Church who has received ecclesiastical preferment, or has graduated at the universities, has indirectly approved of these claims to spiritual authority made and acted on by Henry, Edward and Elizabeth. For every such clergyman takes the Oath of Supremacy, wherein he *solemnly* declares that the Sovereign of the British Isles "is the only *Supreme Governor* of this Realm and of all other of His Highness dominions and countries as well *in all spiritual or ecclesiastical things or causes* as temporal." The taker of such an oath ought to know that such a claim to Spirit-

---

1 Ives: Trials of a Mind, p. 130.

ual jurisdiction has the warranty neither of Scripture nor of Tradition. To the Apostles and their successors, but not to Kings and Rulers was it said by Jesus Christ : "As the Father hath *sent* me so send I you;" "Go teach all nations." Therefore no Act or Acts of Parliament could confer on the Sovereign, power in things *Spiritual*—What would be thought of Congress declaring the President to be possessed of ecclesiastical jurisdiction?

Of this, then, there can be no doubt, even from the few facts adduced, that as truly as the American Colonies withdrew their allegiance from the Sovereign of England and created a new government and centre of authority, so as truly did the Tudor Sovereigns, aided by a subservient Parliament, compel the Church *in* England to reject allegiance to the Roman Pontiff, and made it the Church *of* England, insisting that whatever ecclesiastical or spiritual power it had, flowed from the Crown of England, to which consequently the Church became subject, as any other department of State. Hooker says : "There is required an universal power which reacheth over all, imparting supreme *authority* of government over all courts, all judges, all causes, the operation of which power is as well to strengthen, maintain, and uphold particular jurisdictions, which happily might else be of small effect, as also to remedy that which they are able to help, and to redress that wherein they at any time do otherwise than they ought to do. This power being some time in the Bishop of Rome, who by sinister practices had drawn it into his hands, was for just considerations by public consent annexed unto the King's Royal Seat and Crown." [1] Making every allowance for Hooker's extraordinary hallucination in not apparently realizing that Civil power appertains to the State and Spiritual power to the Church, his statement of the Royal Supremacy in things Spiritual is lucid, and coming from so distinguish an Anglican, has additional weight. It clearly expresses *separation from* and *protest against* the spiritual jurisdiction of the Roman Pontiff. Whether the Bishop of Rome had drawn this spiritual power by sinister practice into his own hands, we have examined previously.

It is unnecessary to follow the efforts made to pervert the doctrines of the Church during the period beginning in 1534, when Henry VIII was voted Spiritual Head of the Church, and ending with 1558, when by Act of Parliament the said Headship was decreed to be perpetual in Elizabeth and her successors. It is sufficient for our purpose to see the decisions concerning faith made in the first Convocation after the Church of England had been fully established by law. Stow tells us that "In the month of June, 1559, the old Bishops of England then living were called and examined by certain of the Queen's Majesty's Council, when the Bishops of York, Ely and London with others to the number of thirteen, for refusing to take the oath touching the Queen's Supremacy and other Articles, were deprived from their Bishoprics." Some of these were committed to prison. Elizabeth proceeded to create another hierarchy.

---

1 Eccles. Pol. VIII., 8, 4.

As Supreme Governor in matters spiritual and ecclesiastical, Her Majesty convoked this new bench of Bishops. They accordingly met in London from both provinces and were presided over by Parker, the Archbishop of Canterbury. Parker had been instituted and invested with metropolitan power by the Queen. The Convocation was therefore duly summoned, it was composed of the newly created teaching body of the Church *of* England, and it possessed in its plentitude, subject to the Sovereign's final approval of its deeds, whatever authority the Crown could confer.

The Articles of Doctrine were taken into serious consideration, they were duly discussed; and finally the Thirty-nine Articles almost in their present form were adopted by Convocation in 1562. They became the legal standard of doctrine, symbol of the newly established Church. Subscription to them by the Clergy was enacted by Parliament in 1570. The Laity are obliged by the 5th Canon of the Church to abstain from asserting that "any of the Nine and Thirty Articles are erroneous or such as may not be subscribed to with a good conscience." By the 36th Canon 1603, the Clergy are required to declare their assent not only to all the Articles and to the Supremacy, but likewise to the Book of Common Prayer; and finally, by Act of Parliament passed in 1662, all beneficiaries are to declare their "unfeigned assent and consent to the use of all things therein contained and prescribed." "His Majesty's Declaration," standing as preface to this new symbol, asserts: "that the Articles of the Church of England do contain

the true doctrine of the Church of England agreeable to
God's Word : which we do therefore ratify and confirm, re-
quiring all our loving subjects to continue in the uniform
profession thereof, and prohibiting the least difference from
the said articles."

Now, interpreting each of the Thirty-nine articles as prescribed in the Declaration of Charles the First, "in the
plain and full meaning thereof, and not to put one's own
sense or comment to be the meaning of the Article, but
take it in the literal and grammatical sense," we see how
thoroughly they are at variance with, and in opposition
to the doctrines taught by St. Augustine which were held
by the Church in England during the nine and a half
centuries preceding the accession of Henry VIII.

In this new Code, the *principle* of an infallible authority
and unerring testimony on which heretofore Christian Revelation had been accepted is rejected, and there is substituted private judgment. The *field* of Revelation is restricted to the Written Word without Apostolic Tradition.
The Sacrifice of the Mass is henceforward to be regarded
as "a blasphemous fable and a dangerous deceit." Its
correlative doctrine of the Real Presence of Transubstan-
tiation is to be held as "repugnant to the plain words of
Scripture." The Sacraments are reduced to two, the other
five being discarded as rather "of the corrupt following of
the Apostles" than as "Sacraments of the Gospel." The
worship of the Blessed Virgin, of the Saints, of Relics, and
the doctrine of Purgatory are all summarily repudiated as
"fond things vainly invented."

The Book of Common Prayer, first put forth in 1549 and settled in its present form in 1562, became the Liturgy of the Church established by Act of Parliament. Compiled in the main from Catholic Missals, it is necessarily saturated with Catholic teaching and is accordingly oftentimes in open contradiction with the Thirty-nine Articles. On one fundamental question, that of a Sacrificing Priesthood, the declarations of the Articles prevailed. In the Book of Common Prayer the Mass became a Communion Service, the Altar a Communion Table and the Real Presence of Christ in the Blessed Sacrament is explicitly and formally denied in the so-called Black Rubric in these terms :

"Whereas it is ordained in this Office for the Administration of the Lord's Supper, that the Communicant should receive the same kneeling; (which order is well meant, for a signification of our humble and grateful acknowledgement of the benefits of Christ therein given to all worthy Receivers, and for the avoiding of such profanation and disorder in the holy Communion, as might otherwise ensue); yet, lest the same kneeling should by any persons, either out of ignorance or infirmity, or out of malice and obstinacy, be misconstrued and depraved; it is hereby declared, That thereby no adoration is intended, or ought to be done, either unto the Sacramental Bread or Wine there bodily received, or unto any Corporal Presence of Christ's natural Flesh and Blood. For the Sacramental Bread and Wine remain still in their very natural substances, and therefore may not be adored; (for that were Idolatry, to be abhorred of the faith-

ful Christians) ; and the natural Body and Blood of our
Saviour Christ are in Heaven, and not here; it being against
the truth of Christ's natural Body to be at one time in more
places than one."

From the forms for "the ordering of priests and bishops," the words expressing the essential work and office of
a priest namely, the offering of sacrifice were deliberately
expunged. It is true that a century later, Convocation did
insert in the form of ordination "*for the office and work of
a Priest ;*" "*for the office and work of a Bishop.*" But this
addition could not restore the lost succession of a Sacrificing Priesthood ; nor did it as a matter of fact prevent the
utter destruction in the Established Communion, and in the
minds of the People of England, of the idea of the Christain
Sacrifice and Altar.

To justify the assumption of Spiritual Supremacy by
Henry VIII, it is asserted that the Pope of Rome had during successive ages *usurped* the universal headship in spiritual matters. To justify the rejection of doctrines held by
the Roman Church and by the Greek Sects, it is necessary
to say that the Church had *corrupted* the Gospel ; or in the
graphic but horrible words of the Homilies : " Laity and
clergy, learned and unlearned, all ages, sects and degrees of
men, women and children of the whole of Christendom had
been at once drowned in abominable idolatry ; and that for
the space of eight hundred years and more." It will be
remarked that this proves too much ; for if it be accepted,

then did "the Gates of Hell prevail against the Church," and Christian Truth was destroyed. See to what straits men are driven to justify their evil deeds and their revolt, against the ' Pillar and Ground of Truth.'

Henceforth to profess the Faith planted by Augustine was penal; it could only be done at the loss of civil rights. It was felony for a foreigner to teach the Faith of our Fathers, and High Treason if it were done by a subject of the Realm. These and sundry other penal laws remained in force till the Emancipation Act of 1829.

They had sent many a martyr to heaven. In the reign of Elizabeth alone, 129 priests, 59 laymen, and 3 women sacrificed their lives rather than deny the Old Faith.

Clearly the Church of England rejected, repudiated and protested against the Faith of Rome as formally as she did against Rome's Spiritual Jurisdiction. Rightly therefore is she designated PROTESTANT. She broke with Rome on Authority and on Doctrine. By her separation she severed herself from the divine jurisdiction of the Catholic Church and lost every claim to Catholicity. "We see," says Cardinal Newman, " in the English Church, I will not merely say no descent from the first ages, and no relationship to the Church in other lands, but we see no Body Politic of any kind, we see nothing more or less than an Establishment, a department of government, or a function or operation of the State—without substance—a mere collection of officials depending on and living in the supreme Civil Power." ‡

‡ Anglican difficulties, p. 5.

Engendered by Henry VIII and brought to maturity in
the early years of Elizabeth's reign the State Church retained
the Cathedrals and Churches and the old divisions into
dioceses and parishes. Outwardly the form was that of the
Old Church, but inwardly the living divine authority was
ended and there was substituted the human power of the
Crown of England. It was a new creation—the "Church of
England."

The Anglican Communion became one aspect of the State
or mode of civil government ; it is responsible for nothing ;
it depends on the will of its supreme power whom it repre-
sents. The consequence is, it has no identity of existence
nor unity of faith.

And as Newman aptly remarks the Church of England
"is as little bound by what it said or did formerly as this
morning's newspaper by its former numbers except as it is
bound by Law. * * * * * Elizabeth boasted that she
tuned her pulpit ; Charles forbade discussions on Predesti-
nation ; George on the Holy Trinity; Victoria allows differ-
ences on Holy Baptism." To this may be added that the
Queen permits irreconcilable divergencies concerning the
Inspiration of Scripture, the Presence of Christ in the Eucharist, and the practice of Confession—all of which, may
be taught or rejected in the Church of England without
danger of expulsion.

Three dynasties, the Tudor, the Stuart and the Hanover-
ian have ruled England since the Establishment was born,
and what naturally might have been expected has come to

pass. It has been well said, "under the Tudors royal authority predominated, under the Stuarts episcopal; Cranmer was type of the one, and Andrewes and Overall of the other. * * * * Elizabeth was despotic, the Stuarts Anglo-Catholic, their successors essentially Protestant. The Tudors required all persons to agree with themselves, the Stuarts with their Bishops, and William of Orange was indifferent what men believed so long as they differed from the Pope."

Her present gracious Majesty, aided by her Privy Council, has on different occasions decided grave controversies of Faith—notably on Baptism, the Eucharist and Confession.

By Letters Patent, like Bulls of Popes, has the Queen created Ecclesiastical hierarchies in her own dominions. Not content with this, beyond the limit of her own dominions has she erected the Anglican Bishopric of Jerusalem, and some other ten Missionary Sees. In virtue of Her Majesty's Commission the Anglican Bishop of Gibraltar exercises a roving jurisdiction on the seaboard of countries around the Mediterranean. Similarly by the same royal authority, the Archbishop of Canterbury exercises pastoral care over the Anglican communities scattered through Northern and Central Europe. By 5 Victoria, Cap. 6, it is enacted that the Archbishop of Canterbury and York may consecrate British subjects or foreigners to be Bishops in foreign countries and it is declared that such "Bishops so consecrated may exercise, within such limits as may from time to time be assigned for that purpose in such foreign countries by Her Majesty, *spiritual jurisdiction* over the ministers of British congregations of the United Church of England and Ireland, and over such other Protestant congregations as may be desirous of placing themselves under their authority." Even were the Queen possessed of such divine spiritual power, this enactment is made ignoring that the intrusion of bishops into the dioceses of others is formally condemned by the first Ecumenical Council of the Church, held at Nice in 325.

The action of the Queen in our own day is a tangible proof that the Supremacy claimed for deciding in doctrinal matters and for confering jurisdiction by the Tudors in the 16th century is vigorously acted on by the Hanoverians in the 19th century.

This exercise of Spiritual Supremacy is by no means an enforced imposition on the Protestant Bishops of England. Assembled in Convocation in 1854, their Lordships voted an address to her present Majesty. Queen Victoria, in these words: "*we not only recognize but highly prize your Majesty's Supremacy in all causes ecclesiastical* over all persons, and every part of your Majesty's Dominions, as it was maintained in ancient times, against the usurpation of the See of Rome, and was recovered and re-asserted at the Reformation."

Indeed the 'Oath of Homage' weds each Bishop of the Established Church in our own day to the Spiritual Supremacy of the Queen. Here is the form : "I, A. B., Doctor in Divinity, now elected Bishop of ——, do hereby declare that your Majesty is the *only supreme* governor of this your

realm *in spiritual and ecclesiastical things,* as well as in temporal, and that no foreign prelate or potentate has any
jurisdiction within this realm; and I acknowledge that I
hold the said bishopric, *as well as the spiritualities* as the
temporalities thereof, *only of your Majesty.* And for the
same temporalities I do my homage presently to your
Majesty. So help me God. God save Queen Victoria."

The Anglican Communion remains as it ever was the
Creature of the State, begotten by Act of Parliament, animated by the civil authority of the Crown, and at the mercy
of Act of Parliament for the continuance of its life.

Here is Cardinal Newman's opinion of it, given in his
Apologia : [1] " I am bound to confess that I felt a great
change in my view of the Church of England. I cannot
tell how soon there came on me—but very soon—an extreme
astonishment that I had ever imagined it to be a portion of
the Catholic Church. For the first time I looked at it from
without, and (as I should myself say) saw it as it was. Forthwith I could not get myself to see in it anything else, than
what I had so long fearfully suspected, from as far back as
1836—a mere national institution. As if my eyes were suddenly opened, so I saw it—spontaneously, apart from any
definite act or reason or any argument ; and so I have seen
it ever since. * * * * When I looked upon the poor
Anglican Church, for which I had labored so hard, and
upon all that appertained to it, and thought of our various

---

1 Apologia p. 339.

attempts to dress it up doctrinally and æsthetically, it seemed
to me to be the veriest of nonentities. Vanity of vanities, all
is vanity. * * * * I am not speaking of the Anglican
Church with disdain though to people I seem contemptuous.
To them it is of course " Aut Cæsar aut nullus, but not to me.
It may be a great creation though it *be* not divine, and this
is how I judge it. * * * * I recognize in the Anglican
Church a time honored institution of noble historical mem-
ories, a monument of ancient wisdom, a momentous arm of
political strength, a great national organ, a source of vast
popular advantage, and, to a certain point a witness and
teacher of religious truth. * * * * But that it is something sacred, that it is an oracle of revealed doctrine, that it
can claim a share in St. Ignatius or St. Cyprian, that it can
take the rank, contest the teaching, and stop the path of the
Church of St. Peter, that it can call itself the ' Bride of the
Lamb,' this is the view of it which simply disappeared from
my mind on my conversion, and which would be almost a
miracle to reproduce. ' I went by and lo ! it was gone ; I
sought it but its place could nowhere be found ; ' and nothing can bring it back to me. And as to its possession of an
Episcopal succession from the time of the Apostles, well, it
may have it, and if the Holy See ever so decide, I will believe it as being the decision of a higher judgment than my
own ; but, for myself I must have St. Philip's gift, who saw
the sacerdotal character on the forehead of a gaily attired
youngster, before I can by own wit acquiesce in it, for anti-
quarian arguments are altogether unequal to the urgency of
visible facts.".

To sum up :—

I. The Established Church of England rejected the divine and spiritual authority of the successors of St. Peter; took in its stead human authority from the Sovereign of England, and so constituted itself a State Department of the Crown.

II. The Established Church of England rejected the divine and therefore infallible teaching authority of the Church; it substituted private judgment; it created the Thirty-nine Articles as the boundary and symbol of its doctrine ; it accepted the Crown, aided later by the Council, which may be composed of men of any or no religion, as the ultimate judge of its doctrine.

III. The result has been that England which for nine centuries believed in *one* Church and had *one* faith, is at present, according to Whitaker's Almanac for this year, split up into some *one hundred and fifty sects.* The Church of England herself boasts of a comprehensiveness ranging from the most attenuated latitudinarinism to the extremest ritualistic doctrine ; and were it not for the iron hand of the State, which grasps her firmly, she would fall to pieces by the warring elements of High, Low and Broad existing within.

IV.

The Protestant Episcopalian Church in the United States is daughter of the Church established by Law in England. The daughter has the same symbol of Faith, the Thirty-nine

Articles ; the same Liturgy, the Book of Common Prayer,
augmented by sundry "Enrichments," toned down by allow-
ing the article in the Apostles' Creed on the Descent into
Hell, to be considered unimportant, by the omission of the
Athanasian Creed, by obliterating almost every trace of
auricular confession, together with the suppression of the
form of absolution from the office of the Visitation of the
Sick. She has her doctrine, her discipline, her worship
from the English Establishment. In common with her
Mother she *protests* against the supremacy of St. Peter and
his successors ; she *protests* against the teaching brought
from Rome by Augustine. Rightly therefore does the
daughter bear the name PROTESTANT. She holds no communion with Rome ; she has no jurisdiction from the See of
Peter ; consequently she forms no part of the Organic Body
of Christ, nor indeed of any other organism, for, like her
Mother, and apart from that Mother, she forms a separate
and independent Corporation possessed of human authority
and bereft of every shred of the divine jurisdiction which
appertains to the Catholic Church.

There are of her pastors a limited but increasing number
who, relying on the Book of Common Prayer and ignoring
the Thirty-nine Articles to which they *ex animo* pledged
themselves by oath, teach in contradiction to the Doctrinal
Code of their Communion, the characteristic doctrines of
the Catholic Church. These clergymen insist on a blind
obedience to their teaching and direction, the like of which
is unknown in the Church which claims the gift of infallibil-

ity. Some go so far as to exact a *vow of obedience to their injunctions.* These call themselves Catholic, and stigmatize as Protestant their brother clergy and bishops who are pleased to follow the more logical procedure of taking doctrine from the Articles, to explain the devotional expressions of the Prayer Book. But to arrogate the name Catholic does not generate Catholicity. None are louder in their denunciation of an "Infallible Pope" than are holders of these tenets. Surely they ought to realize that they themselves *act* as though they are the unerring expounders of the Book of Common Prayer and of the Articles. They ought to know that Bishops and not priests constitute the "Ecclesia docens." The words of St. Ignatius, of the second century, are as true now as then. He says: "Apart from the Bishop it is neither lawful to baptize nor to hold an agape; but whatever he judges right, that also is well pleasing unto God, that all which is done may be safe and sure."[1] Clergymen who act otherwise must not be surprised that men of common sense finally prefer subjection to one canonically elected Pope, instead of to many self-constituted Popes.

In one particular the absence of Catholicity in the Protestant Episcopal Church of the United States is more patent than in her Mother. For the English Church at least claims authority, whatever be its nature, from the Sovereign; but her American daughter draws hers from nowhere. She is an authority to herself. Allow for the sake

---

1 Ep. ad Smyr. n. 8.

of argument that her Orders derived from Scotland and
England are valid—a fact extremely dubious, seeing that in
our own day a large number of the Anglican clergy holding
benefices in England, alarmed by the evidence brought
against their Orders, have been not only re-ordained but
conditionally baptized, re-confirmed, and have secured some
five properly consecrated bishops who actively continue this
work of re-ordination. Admit the validity of the orders,
whence does the Protestant Episcopal Church of the United
States derive its mission and jurisdiction?

The Sovereign of England claimed a century ago to
be the fountain head of spiritual jurisdiction only within the
British Realm. In the reign of the present Queen, Parliament has given greater extension to this claim. Previous to
the Independence there were no Anglican bishops in the
present United States. The only supervision of the clergy
was done by the Bishop of London, appointed by the Sovereign of England to be overseer of the Colonies.

The Independence of the United States was declared in
the July of 1776; and with it the authority temporal and
spiritual of the Sovereign of England ceased to be in the
States. Consequently the clergy of the Church of England
under the new national sovereignty had no spiritual authority.
There were no bishops, and therefore there was no church.
This state of things continued for eight years, when Dr.
Seabury was consecrated in Scotland in November, 1784.
In the February of 1787, two others, White and Provost,
were consecrated bishops in London. These held a con-

vention in the October of 1789, and formed themselves into
a corporate body. They gave it the name of the Protestant
Episcopal Church in the United States of America; they
created a constitution for this corporate body; they revised
the Book of Common Prayer according to the new political
position, and ordered it in this revised form to be used from
the first of October 1790.

The time of the creation of the Protestant Episcopal
Church in the United States is thus determined to be seven-
teen and a half centuries after the birth of the "Body of
Christ," the Church of the Living God.

It could not have received jurisdiction from England;
there is no pretension that jurisdiction was obtained from
the President of the United States, who by the way has as
much right to accord it as has the Sovereign of England.
Clearly therefore the authority of the Protestant Episcopal
Church has no origin outside of itself. It is a corporation
possessed of such powers as its own members may create,
define and accept. This authority is but human, and
depends for extension, restriction, existence and validity on
the will of the majority. The complete autonomy of the
Protestant Episcopal Church is secured. Its government
is not even one with its English mother; for in an evil
moment it introduced lay representation, " an unfortunate
example, set in a bad time," wrote the late Doctor Pusey.
This isolation of the " Protestant Episcopal Church " de-
prives it of Catholicity, and makes it stand to the Church
of Christ in the same relation that the United States do to
England, namely, separated and independent.

The position of the " Protestant Episcopal Church " is, so
far as self-government is concerned, one with that of the
"Methodist Episcopal Church." John Wesley was but a
presbyter of the Anglican Communion. He without any
sanction of the Established Church, and much against his
will, called into existence another corporation or sect differ-
ing in doctrine and government. The Church of England
had been separated from Rome not more than two centuries, and already were the poor neglected and the middle
class lost to the National Establishment. Indeed it has
to be added, they have never been regained. Wesley was
deeply moved by their spiritual wants. He labored very
earnestly and was pre-eminently successful. It is said that
before his death his followers numbered 80,000.

Wesley perceived that the consequence of American Independence to his followers would be the formation of an independent Society. To meet the emergency Wesley convinced
himself that presbyter and bishop were one and the same
order in the early ages of the Church. And thereupon he
laid hands on, and set aside Coke as bishop of the nascent
community of Methodists in the States. Of this mode of
creating Episcopal orders, there is no need of discussion
here. For our purpose it is sufficient to know that Coke
came in Wesley's name and with Wesley's authority to the
Conference at Baltimore in 1784 to announce that a separate
and independent Methodist Church might be created under
Episcopal rule.

The organization was formed, the body has grown and

prospered. It has numerically fourfold as many clergy and six times as many laity as have the Protestant Episcopalians. The spiritual authority to which it lays claim, is derived from no external source, it was begotten by its own clergy and can be restricted, extended or destroyed by the acts of the Body. The authority is indubitably human.

The "Protestant Episcopal Church" of the United States has no other title to its authority in things spiritual. It cannot produce any credentials to show that it derives authority from the living Mystic Body of Christ.

In common with its Methodist sister it can claim only that authority which was created by its members, an authority purely human, not divine. At the Convention one of the speakers, Mr. Stewart, is reported to have said: "Is this Church to call itself '*the Catholic Church*' of the United States? Was it universal? He thought that the proposition savored a good deal of vanity. He thought that it would be an act of assumption which would render them ridiculous in the eyes of the religious and civilized world."

Rev. Dr. Fulton, in the course of the same debate is reported to have said that "He lived in a city of 350,000 inhabitants, and he did not think the church had more than 2,500 communicants there. Honestly computed he supposed that the whole membership of the Protestant Episcopal Church in this country was not more than *two per cent.* of the population. It might be *three per cent.* but he doubted it. * * * * In view of the single fact which he had mentioned, would it be modest or truthful to call the

Protestant Episcopalian *The Holy Catholic Church* of the
United States of America ?"

Whereas, "The Church" has been shown to be an Organism vivified by the Holy Ghost and as incapable of
Division as is the human body;

Whereas, "The Church" was commissioned with divine
power for the Ministry of the Gospel;

Whereas, "Catholic" has been shown to signify continuous
identity of life from the day of Pentecost, universal ex-
pansion with close intercommunion of all the organs and
members, and possession of the whole deposit of 'the
Faith once delivered to the Saints':

And seeing that, "The Protestant Episcopalian Church"
is a corporation with a separate autonomy self constituted and self named;

Seeing that "The Protestant Episcopalian Church" is possessed of no other than the human power which its
members create;

Seeing that "the Protestant Episcopalian Church" constituted itself a corporation in 1789, and accepted the
Thirty-nine Articles decreed to be the legal doctrinal
code of the National Church of England in 1562:

Then may we answer Dr. Fulton's question: it is not
"modest or truthful" to call 'the Protestant Episcopal
Church' *the Holy Catholic Church.*

"*The Holy Catholic Church*" admitted by the general consent of men to be the Mother and Mistress of Churches, is the Roman Church which planted the Faith in Roman Britain, then in Saxon England and established there thirteen centuries ago a Hierarchy of Order and Jurisdiction, and which a second time, in 1850, erected the Hierarchy for the small remnant who notwithstanding three centuries of persecution, stood throughout true to the Old Faith. The Roman Church did, as soon as America was discovered, duly commission her Priests to bear to the new continent the light of the Gospel. The proclamation made to the natives by the pioneer discoverers bears these remarkable words: "the Church: the Queen and Sovereign of the World."

Columbus and his crew having been absolved after confession, received the Blessed Sacrament, heard Holy Mass, and embarked in the Santa Maria and two small vessels. Night and morning from off the unknown deep did they chant *Ave Maris Stella*. When the long-looked for land hove in sight, the indomitable Columbus and his now joyous crew on bended knee sang *Te Deum* to God the Mighty. Next day, Oct. 14, 1492, Columbus as Lord High Admiral, and bearing the Royal Standard of Spain, landed, and in the beautiful words of Washington Irving, "threw himself upon his knees, kissed the earth and returned thanks to God with tears of joy. Then rising, he drew his sword, displayed the royal standard and took possession in the names of the Castilian Sovereigns." The

soil and island he consecrated with the name of the Holy
Redeemer, San Salvador.

Columbus returned to Spain, and on his next journey
across the Atlantic, he brought with him a Vicar-Apostolic
and twelve priests. These erected their first church at
Isabella, Hayti in 1494. This may be regarded as the occasion when 'the Church, One, Holy, Catholic and Roman'
was planted in America. She is the oldest institution on
the new continent, and from the day of her establishment
has ever increased. She has steadily raised her altars,
augmented her priests, and has thus secured to an ever increasing number of places the Sacrifice according to the
Order of Melchisidec.

Along the seaboard, from the West Indies down to Cape
Horn, thence up the whole of the Pacific Coast to Beh-
ring's Straits, inland into South America, into Mexico and
among the Aborigines, did missionaries armed with the authority of Rome, erect the cross and preach the glad tidings
of salvation. The very names of the towns bear evidence
to the faith of the colonists. " The Dominicans, Franciscans, and Jesuits of Spain share between them the South
from Florida to California; the Recollects and Jesuits of
France traverse the country in every direction, from the
mouth of the St. Lawrence to the shores of the Pacific,
and from the Gulf of Mexico to Hudson's Bay; and finally,
the English Jesuits plant the Cross for a time amid the
tribes of Maryland, during the short time of Catholic
supremacy in that colony. The Spaniards were the first to

preach the Gospel in the territory now actually comprised in the United States."[1]

Within fifty years of discovery, America could count her martyrs, her bishops and dioceses. In 1529 the See of Sta. Marta in New Granada was erected; in 1531 that of Caraccas in Venezuela; in 1539 that of Lima; in 1551 that of Chiquisca in Bolivia; in 1561 at Santiago; in 1561 at Bahia in the Brazils; in 1570 at Cordova in the Argentine Republic.

In North America the soil was well purpled with the blood of martyr missionaries. The Indian tribes along and around the Rio Grande were Catholics before England had planted Virginia or New England. California and Texas had been evangelized under the Spaniards by the Franciscans. And in Bancroft's words: "The religious zeal of the French bore the cross to the banks of the St. Mary and the confines of Lake Superior, and looked wistfully towards the homes of the Sioux in the Valley of the Mississippi, five years before the New England Eliot had addressed the tribe of Indians that dwelt within six miles of Boston harbor." The story of Father Marquette, and the work of himself and his Jesuit companions in the Valley of the Mississippi, are household words. The conquest of Mexico was followed by the formation of a diocese. With the expedition of Narvaez in 1528 into Florida were missionaries, one of whom, Juan Juarez, was appointed by the

---

1. See Mr. Gilmary Shea's most interesting "New Hist. of Cath. Ch. in the United States," and Mr. W. H. Sadlier's admirable School History of the United States.

Pope, Bishop of Florida. He was the first Bishop within the limits of the present United States. Sees were erected in Montreal and Quebec in 1659 and 1674.

It will be remembered that the Church of England was established or created in 1533,—that is *five years after the first Catholic Bishop* was appointed to Florida, and the "Protestant Episcopalian Church" does not appear as a corporate body *till two hundred and sixty years later.* An English expedition landed at the site of the present Jamestown, May 13, 1607, on which occasion Revd. Dr. May, a member of the party, and clergyman of the Church of England, administered communion ; probably this was the second time the Anglican rite was performed on American soil. The first occasion was by Master Wolfall in Frobisher's Expedition of 1578, which failed to get a footing. After the settlement of Virginia, Sir George Yeardly convened the first Legislative Assembly. It enacted immediately that the Church of England should be established in the colony; and measures were taken for the formation of a convention of clergy. The first was held in 1621, and from the account left, there were in the whole colony only five clergymen. The Bishop of London, England, undertook to procure others. In 1680 Dr. Compton another Bishop of London had an inquiry instituted concerning the state of the Church of England in the colonies. It was shown that there were *only four Anglican ministering clergymen in the whole of the English colonies in North America*, and this at a time when the Roman Church was firmly planted.

Since the Declaration of Independence the current of immigration has brought a host of Catholics to the Eastern seaboard of North America fleeing before persecution or seeking in a new land the fortune denied them in their own countries. Of all nations and tribes, and peoples, they are one in the blessed gift of Faith. They are independent witnesses from every clime of the uniform doctrine of the Roman Church, though taught in many tongues.

It is said that in the two Americas there are at present fifty-five million Catholics under the spiritual government of one hundred and ninety Bishops and Vicars Apostolic. Of these about eight millions are in the United States. They are governed by Pastors constituted by the Roman Pontiff in hierarchical order. The first diocese was created in 1789; and now ten archiepiscopal provinces having seventy-one Bishops and six thousand eight hundred Priests, form the great and ONLY ARTERY through which divine spiritual authority in faith, morals and discipline flows from the fountain-head, the See of Peter, to the inhabitants of the United States.

As citizens of the great American Republic joyfully do Catholics render obedience, for conscience sake, to the authorities that be. They rejoice and gratefully acknowledge there is neither let nor hindrance in the exercise of their religion. In their conduct they show that while permitted to render freely to God and His Church, their service, they the more heartily render to Cæsar the things that are Cæsar's. They are for this reason a solid moral power in the States.

Time will fuse them into a great American Catholic people.

On the other hand, their unity of faith, their obedience to pastors, their attachment to Holy Church, their many institutions founded mainly by the generous sacrifices of the poor, their undying efforts to secure religious education: are so many tongues loudly proclaiming to all the presence and the living power of the Church One, Holy, Catholic and Roman in the United States. *

The hearts of these millions of Catholics earnestly long and pray that all their fellow-citizens may enter and be of the One Fold. Faithful Catholics, masters and servants, poor and rich, day by day appeal to the Throne of Mercy that light to know the truth, and strength to follow it, may be given to all Americans, but more especially to those with whom they are brought in personal contact.

The pastors of the nascent church in the States placed, with the approval of Rome, the country under the patronage of Mary Immaculate anxious that her Son may be served in spirit and in truth on a soil which is not sullied by its people having revolted against the Church and her doctrine. They repeat to the Episcopalians of the United States as S. Augustine of Hippo, did to the Donatists of North Africa, who prided themselves on their religious national unity, and relied on the number and succession of their Bishops : " Come, brethren, if you wish to be inserted in the vine ; for we grieve when we see

---

* The Methodist Convention now sitting passed a resolution to send Missionaries among these as among the heathen

you lie thus, cut off from it. Number the Bishops from the very Seat of Peter, and in that list of fathers see what has been the succession ; this is the rock against which the proud gates of hell do not prevail."

The world without stigmatizes this Church, in bad grammar, "*Romish and foreign.*" It is an appeal to the passions of the people. Do those who so speak forget that Jesus Christ and his twelve Apostles were of the Jewish race, and therefore *foreigners?* Obedience of the children of the Church in matters spiritual to the fountain-head of authority, the Holder of which may be of any nationality residing in Rome, is no more *foreign* than is obedience to the Apostles, who abode in Palestine. As we have seen, the Church of Christ is to be universal, and not national ; therefore in her nothing can be foreign.

In calling the Church *Roman* it is not by way of contrast to " Protestant Episcopal," to " English," to " Methodist," to " Anglo or Old Catholics." The term is used to express the source whence all divine authority flows to every part of the Church. As the historian Lingard has well said : " There is nothing offensive in this appellation, as in other names with which we are frequently honored. If, then, we refuse to adopt it, the reason is, because it imports what is irreconcilable with our principles, that Churches which have separated from the ancient Catholic Church may still have a right to the title of Catholic."[1]
On this ground did Cardinal Consalvi at the Congress of

Psalm C. Don S. Aug 1 and 7.

Vienna object to ' Roman Catholic ' and asked for ' Catholic and Roman.' We have in the Church those who on account of nationalism or ritual receive special names, such as the Maronites, the Melchites, and others. But all are subject to the Pope, profess their belief in the Roman Chuch, and they are in communion with every part of the Church.

And it has to be remembered " Roman " is not of yesterday, though persecution has necessitated accentuating the name in certain countries in our times.

" It will be anticipated," [2] says Newman, " that the duration of error had not the faintest tendency to deprive the ancient Church of the West of the title of Catholic ; and it is needless to produce evidence of a fact which is on the very face of the history. The Arians seem never to have claimed the Catholic name. *It is more than remarkable that the Catholics during this period*" (that is, from the beginning of the fifth to the end of the sixth century) "*were denoted by the additional title of 'Romans.'* Of this there are many proofs in the history of St. Gregory of Tours, Victor of Vite, and the Spanish Councils. * * * This appellation had two meanings; one which will readily suggest itself, is its use in contrast to the word 'barbarian' as denoting the faith of the Empire, as 'Greek'

---

1 Catechism, p. 35. 2 Development, p. 729.

occurs in St. Paul's Epistle. In this sense it would more naturally be used by the Romans themselves than by others. * * * * But the word certainly contains also an allusion to the faith and communion of the Roman See. In this sense the Emperor Theodosius, in his letter to Accasius of Berœa, contrasts it with Nestorianism, which was within the Empire as well as Catholicism; during the controversy raised by that heresy, he exhorts him and others to shew themselves '*approved priests of the Roman religion.*'" Newman continues citing facts and phrases from several authors, among others the Emperor Gratian and St. Jerome, so as to support his statement. It would be too long to quote these in full; the following will suffice for the purposes of this pamphlet.

"The chief ground of the Vandal Huneric's persecution of the African Catholics seems to have been their connection with their brethren beyond the sea, which he looked at with jealousy as *introducing a foreign power into his territory.* Prior to this he had published an edict calling on the Homöusian Bishops (for on this occasion he did not call them Catholics) to meet his own bishops at Carthage, and treat concerning the Faith that 'their meetings to the seduction of Christian souls might not be held in the provinces of the Vandals.' Upon this invitation Eugenius of Carthage replied that all transmarine Bishops of the Orthodox Communion ought to be summoned, 'in particular because it is a matter for the whole world, not special to the African provinces,' that 'they could not undertake a

point of faith *sine universitatis assensu.*' Huneric answered
that if Eugenius would make him sovereign of *the orbis
terrarum* he would comply with his request. This led
Eugenius to say that the orthodox faith was 'the only
true faith;' that the king ought to write to his allies
abroad, if he wished to know it; and that he himself
would write to his brethren for foreign bishops, 'who,'
he says, 'may assist us in setting before you the true
faith, common to them and to us, and *especially to the
Roman Church, which is the head of all Churches.*' More-
over the African Bishops in their banishment to Sardinia,
to the number of sixty, with S. Fulgentius at their head,
quote with approbation the words of Pope Hormisdas, to
the effect that they hold on ʻthe point of free will and
divine grace what *the Roman, that is the Catholic, Church*
follows and preserves." * * * *

" Nor was the association of Catholicism with the See
of Rome an introduction of that age. The Emperor Gratian, in the fourth century, had ordered that the Churches,
which the Arians had usurped, should be restored (not to
those who held 'the Catholic faith,' or 'the Nicene creed,'
or were 'in communion with the orbis terrarum ') but '*who
chose the communion of Damasus,' the then Pope.* It was St.
Jerome's rule also in some well-known passages. Writing
against Ruffinus, who had spoken of ' OUR FAITH,' he says:
What does he mean by 'his faith'? That which is the
strength of *the Roman Church,* or that which is contained
in the works of Origen ? If he answer '*the Roman,' then*

we are Catholics who have borrowed nothing of Origen's error; but if Origen's blasphemy be his faith, then while he is charging me with inconsistency he proves himself to be an 'heretic.' The other passage is still more exactly to the point, because it was written on occasion of a schism. The divisions at Antioch had thrown the Catholic Church into a remarkable position; there were two bishops in the See—one in connection with the East, the other with Egypt and the West—with which was there 'Catholic Communion.' St. Jerome had no doubt on the subject. Writing to St. Damasus he says: 'Since the East tears into pieces the Lord's coat, * * * therefore by me is *the chair of Peter to be consulted*, and that faith which is prized *by the Apostles mouth.* * * * Though your greatness terrifies me, yet your kindness invites me. From the Priest I ask the salvation of the victim, from the Shepherd the protection of the sheep. Let us speak without offense: I court not the Roman height: I speak with the successor of the Fisherman and the disciple of the Cross. I who follow none as my chief but Christ, *am associated in communion with thy blessedness, that is, with the See of Peter.* On the rock the Church is built. Whoso shall eat the Lamb *outside that House is profane.* * * * I know not this Vatalis ' (the Apolinarian); ' Meletius I reject; I am ignorant of Paulinus. Whoso gathereth not with thee, scattereth; that is, he who is not of Christ is of Anti-Christ.' Again, ' The ancient authority of the monks dwelling round about, rises against me; I meanwhile cry out, *if any be joined to Peter's chair he is mine.*' "

"Here was what may be considered a *dignus vindice nodus*, the Church being divided, and an arbiter wanted. Such a case had also occurred in Africa in the controversy with the Donatists. Four hundred bishops, though in but one region, were a fifth part of the whole Episcopate of Christendom, and might seem too many for a schism, and in themselves too large a body to be cut off from God's inheritance by a mere majority, even had it been overwhelming. St. Augustine, then, who so often appeals to the *orbis terrarum*, sometimes adopts a more prompt criterion. He tells certain Donatists to whom he writes that the Catholic Bishop of Carthage " was able to make light of the thronging multitude of his enemies, when he found himself by letters of credence joined *both to the Roman Church, in which ever had flourished the principality of the Apostolical See*, and to the other lands whence the gospel came to Africa itself."

And Newman concludes : " There are good reasons then for explaining the Gothic and Arian use of the word ' Roman,' when applied to the Catholic Church and faith, of something beyond its mere connection with the Empire, which the barbarians were assaulting ; nor would ' Roman ' surely be the most obvious word to denote the orthodox faith, in the mouths of a people who had learned their heresy from a Roman Emperor and Court."

In unmistakable terms do the voices of these great servants of God come to us from the fourth and fifth centuries declaring the One Holy Catholic Apostolic Church to *be Roman.*

And the Old Church of St. Augustine planted in England gives no uncertain note. The voice of St. Aldhelm, first Bishop of Sherbun in England, who died 709 proclaims: "To conclude everything in the casket of one short sentence. In vain of the Catholic faith do they vainly boast, who follow not the teaching and rule of St. Peter. For the foundation of the Church and ground of the faith primarily in Christ and then in Peter, unrocked by the stress of tempests, shall not waver, the Apostle so pronouncing (1 Cor. iii, 11 ;) other foundation no one can lay besides that which is laid, which is Jesus Christ. But to Peter has the Truth thus sanctioned the Church's privilege (Matt. xvi.) 'Thou art Peter, and upon his this Rock I will build my Church."

And Alcuin the most distinguished English scholar of the latter half of the Eighth century writes : "Lest he be found to be a schismatic or a non-Catholic, let him follow the most approved authority of the Roman Church, that whence we have received the seeds of the Catholic faith that we may find the exemplars of salvation, lest the members be severed from the head, lest the Key-bearer of the Heavenly Kingdom exclude such as he shall recognize as alien from his teaching." [1]

And St. Anselm, the famous scholastic philosopher and Archbishop of Canterbury, who died in 1089, informs us : "It is certain that he who does not obey the ordinances of the Roman Pontiff, which are issued for the maintenance of

---

1 Ep. 75.

the Christian religion, is disobedient to the Apostle Peter, whose Vicar he is, nor is he of that flock which was given to him (Peter) by God. Let him then find some other gates of the Kingdom of Heaven, for by those he shall not go in, of which the Apostle Peter holds the Keys." [1]

And the holy abbot of Ridal in Yorkshire, St. Aelred, whom Butler says died in 1167, earnestly exhorts : [2] "Brethren, let no one seduce you with vain words. Let no one say to you, Lo here is Christ, or there, since Christ ever abides in the faith of Peter, which the Holy Roman Church has especially received from Peter, and retains in the Rock, which is Christ. * * * Of this Church Peter was the first Prince, to whom it was said, 'Upon this Rock I will build My Church ;' and again, 'Feed My sheep :' and again, 'To thee will I give the keys of the kingdom of heaven, and whatsoever thou shalt bind upon earth shall be bound too in heaven,' and the rest. This is the Church which the Holy Apostle calls of the first-born, the plentitude of whose power in the person of its Prince passing over from the East to the West by the authority of the Holy Spirit established itself in the Roman Church. * * * This is the Roman Church, with whom he who communicates not is a heretic. To her it belongs to advise all, to judge of all, to provide for all, to whom in Peter that word was addressed, 'And thou, some time converted, confirm thy brethren.' Whatsoever she decrees I

---

1 Lib. iv., Ep. xiii. 2 Serm. 33—cited from Ryder's Catholic Controversy.

receive ; I approve what she approves ; what she condemns
I condemn."

In the nineteenth century in the days in which we live
the Roman Church is *One* : (1)—All her members, though
of all tongues, and political parties, and forms of government, are united in closest communion under the Visible
Head, who, together with the *one* Episcopate held by the
successors of the Apostolic College—the Bishops dis-
persed through the whole communion, whom the Holy
Ghost appoints—rule and govern this Body Politic, this
living Organization. (2)—There is *one* and the same principle of faith, namely, divine authority and testimony for
one body of doctrines held by her pastors and people
individually and collectively. (3)—There is *one* sacramental system and worship, receiving the same explanation
and producing the same effects in the possession of all
her children.

The Roman Church is *Holy :* (1) Because her doctrine is
in itself holy, ever inviting men to ascend higher and higher
in virtue. (2) She is *holy* because she has begotten a mighty
army of heroic saints. and martyrs, and virgins. On every
soil has she planted and founded institutions created and
directed by those who wishing to be perfect, give up home
and wealth to labor for their Master in suffering humanity.
(3) She is *holy* because consumed by the desire to enkindle
the fire of divine love on earth ; she is instant in season,
and out of season in preaching the gospel to those who are
in sin or in darkness. The glory of converting Pagan na-

tions is hers. This no Protestant sect, backed by illimited wealth or the greatest political power, has ever been able to accomplish.

The Roman Church is *Catholic:* (1) because she is of no one nation and in her constitution and her teaching she is fitted to all peoples and forms of government. (2) Because her principle of faith is applicable to all, young and old, learned and unlearned. (3) Because her identity of existence from Pentecost day till now can be plainly traced. (4) Because she alone has the whole of Revelation—the Faith delivered to the saints. Circumstances have obliged her to formulate the Faith in dogmatic decisions and creeds so as to bear witness to what is contained in the *deposit* of faith ; but such authoritative declarations are no additions to the Faith, they do but unwrap what it contains and explicitly expose its separate doctrines. (5) Because she admits of no rival; she is ever aggressive, condemning schism and heresy; by friend and by foe she is known as THE CATHOLIC CHURCH.

The tide of indifference, of agnosticism, of infidelity, of socialism, of civil disorder is rapidly rising. God's Church can alone stem it. Numbers and influence and wealth co-operating with the Spouse of Christ can help to do great things to aid in saving humanity from the growing ills. She is the Church of your Baptism, to whom you owe allegiance and obedience; for the saving waters of regeneration are the portal to but one Church. They made you not members of Protestantism, but children of the Church of God.

To you then who fondly believe your religious society to be Catholic, and wish it to be so called, allow me to address, in sincerest affection, the earnest Apostolic words of Pius IX. of glorious memory :

"We conjure and beseech you, with all the warmth of our zeal, and in all charity, to consider and seriously examine whether you follow the path marked out for you by Jesus Christ our Lord, which leads to eternal salvation. No one can deny or doubt that Jesus Christ himself, in order to apply the fruit of His redemption to all generations of men, built His only Church in this world on Peter; that is to say, the Church, One, Holy, Catholic and Apostolic ; and that He gave to it all the necessary power, that the deposit of faith might be preserved whole and inviolable, and that the same faith might be taught to all peoples, kindreds and nations ; that through baptism, all men might become members of this Mystical Body, and that the new life of grace without which no one can ever merit and attain to life eternal might always be preserved and perfected in them ; and that this same Church which is His Mystical Body might always remain in its own nature, firm and immovable to the end of time ; that it might flourish and supply to all its children all the means of salvation.

"Now, whoever will carefully examine and reflect upon the condition of the various religious societies, divided among themselves. and separated from the Catholic Church, which from the days of our Lord Jesus Christ and his Apostles, has never ceased to exercise by its lawful pastors, and still continue, to exercise, the divine power committed to it by this same Lord ; cannot fail to satisfy himself that neither any one of these societies by itself, nor all of them together, can in any manner constitute and be that One Catholic Church which our Lord built and established, and willed should continue ; and that they cannot in any way be said to be branches or parts of that Church, since they are visibly cut off from Catholic unity.

" For, whereas such societies are destitute of that living authority established by God, which especially teaches men what is of faith, and what the rules of morals, and directs and guides them in all those things which pertain to eternal salvation ; so they have continually varied in their doctrines, and this change and variation is ceaselessly going on among them.

" Every one must perfectly understand, and clearly and evidently see, that such a state of things is directly opposed to the nature of the Church instituted by our Lord Jesus Christ ; for in that Church truth must always continue firm and ever inaccessable to all change, as a deposit given to that Church to be guided in its integrity, for the guardianship of which the presence and aid of the Holy Ghost have been promised to the Church forever."

PART II.

I.

ST. CYPRIAN

ON THE UNITY OF THE CHURCH.

———

For as much as the Lord warns us, saying, *Ye are the salt of the earth,* and bids us to possess an innocent simplicity, yet being simple, to be also prudent, is it not befitting, dearest brethren, to hold ourselves in wariness, and by keeping watch with an anxious heart, to become forewarned and withal forearmed, against the snares of our subtle enemy? lest we, who have put on Christ, the Wisdom of God the Father, should yet be found to lack wisdom, for the making sure of our salvation. That persecution is not the only one to be feared, which advances by open assault to the ruin and downfall of God's servants; caution is easy, where the danger is manifest; and the mind is in readiness for the battle, when the enemy makes himself known. More to be feared and more to be watched is a foe, who creeps upon us unawares, who deceives under the image of peace, and glides forward with those stealthy movements, which hath given him the name of Serpent. Such always is his deceitfulness; such the dark and backward artifices, by which he compasses man; thus in the first beginning of the world he wrought his deceit, and by lying words of flattery, led away unformed souls in their incautious credulity. Thus when he would tempt the Lord Himself, he came unawares upon Him, as if to creep on him a second

time and deceive; yet he was seen through and driven
back: beaten down was he, by reason that he was discovered and exposed. Herein is the example given us, to flee
from the way of the old man, and to tread in the footsteps
of Christ who conquered; lest we slide back by incaution
into the toil of death, instead of, through foresight of danger, partaking the immortality that has been gained for us.
Yet how can we partake immortality, unless we keep those
commandments of Christ, by which death is taken prisoner
and overcome? For Himself admonishes us, and says, *If
thou will enter into life, keep the commandments;* and again,
*If ye do the things I command you, henceforth I call you not
servants but friends.* It is such persons, in fine, that He
declares to be stable and enduring; founded in massive
strength upon a rock, and settled with firmness untroubled
and untouched, amidst all the storms and winds of this
world. *Whosever,* saith He, *heareth these sayings of Mine
and doeth them, I will liken him unto a wise man, that built
his house upon a rock ; the rain descended, the floods came, the
winds blew, and beat upon that house, and it fell not, for it
was founded upon a rock.* We ought therefore to have our
footing in His words, to learn and to do all that He taught
and did. But how can he say he believes in Christ,
who does not that which Christ has bade him do? or how
come to the reward of faith, who will keep no faith with the
commandment? Needs must he totter and fall astray;
caught by a spirit of terror, he will be wafted up like dust

in a whirlwind ; nor will his walk lead forward to salvation, who does not hold the truth of the saving way.

2. We must be warned then, dearest brethren, not only against things open and manifest, but also against those which deceive us, through the guile of craft and fraud. What now can be more crafty, or what more artful, than for this enemy, detected and downfallen by the advent of Christ, now that light is come to the nations, and the beams of salvation shine forth unto the health of man, that the deaf may hear the sound of spiritual grace, the blind may open their eyes upon God, the sick regain the strength of an eternal healing, the lame run to church, the dumb lift on high their voices to speak and worship, for him, thus seeing his idols left, his seats and temples deserted by the manifold congregation of believers, to invent the new deceit, whereby to carry the incautious into error, while retaining the name of the Christian profession? He has made heresies and schisms, wherewith to subvert faith, to corrupt truth, and rend unity. Those whom he cannot detain in the blindness of the old way, he compasses and deceives by misleading them on their new journey. He snatches men from out the Church itself, and while they think themselves come to the light, and escaped from the night of this world, he secretly gathers fresh shadows upon them; so that standing neither with the Gospel of Christ, nor with His ordinances, nor with His law, they yet call themselves Christians, walking among darkness, and thinking that they have light; while the foe flatters and misleads, transforms him-

self, according to the word of the Apostle, into *an Angel of light*, and garbs his ministers like ministers of righteousness: these are the maintainers of night for day, of death for salvation, giving despair while they proffer hope, faithlessness clothed as faith, Antichrist under the name of Christ; that by putting false things under an appearance of true, they may with subtilty impede the truth.

3. This will be, most dear brethren, so long as there is no regard to the source of truth, no looking to the Head, nor keeping to the doctrine of our heavenly Master. If any one consider and weigh this, he will not need length of comment or argument. Proof is ready for belief in a short statement of the truth. The Lord saith unto Peter, *I say unto thee,* (saith He) *that thou art Peter, and upon this rock I will build my Church, and the gates of Hell shall not prevail against it. And I will give unto thee the keys of the kingdom of heaven, and whatsoever thou shalt bind on earth, shall be bound also in heaven, and whatsoever thou shalt loose on earth, shall be loosed in heaven.* To him again, after His resurrection, He says, *Feed My sheep.* Upon him being one He builds His Church; and though He gives to all the Apostles an equal power, and says, *As My Father sent Me, even so send I you; receive ye the Holy Ghost: whosoever sins ye remit, they shall be remitted to him, and whosoever sins ye retain, they shall be retained;*—yet in order to manifest unity, He has by His own authority so placed the source of the same unity, as to begin from one. Certainly the other Apostles also were what Peter was, endued with an equal

fellowship both of honour and power; but a commencement
is made from unity, that the Church may be set before us
as one; which one Church, in the Song of Songs, doth the
Holy Spirit design and name in the Person of our Lord :
*My dove, My spotless one, is but one ; she is the only one of her
mother, elect of her that bare her.*

4. He who holds not this unity of the Church, does he
think that he holds the faith? He who strives against and
resists the Church, is he assured that he is in the Church ?
For the blessed Apostle Paul teaches this same thing, and
manifests the sacrament of unity thus speaking ; *There is
One Body, and One Spirit, even as ye are called in One Hope of
your calling ; One Lord, One Faith, One Baptism, One God.*
This unity firmly should we hold and maintain, especially
we Bishops, presiding in the Church, in order that we may
approve the Episcopate itself to be one and undivided. Let
no one deceive the Brotherhood by falsehood ; no one corrupt the truth of our faith, by a faithless treachery. The
Episcopate is one; it is a whole, in which each enjoys full
possession. The Church is likewise one, though she be
spread abroad, and multiplies with the increase of her progeny: even as the sun has rays many, yet one light ; and
the tree boughs many, yet its strength is one, seated in the
deep-lodged root; and as, when many streams flow down
from one source, though a multiplicity of waters seems diffused from the bountifulness of the overflowing abundance,
unity is preserved in the source itself. Part a ray of the
sun from its orb, and its unity forbids this division of light;

break a branch from the tree, once broken it can bud no more; cut the stream from its fountain, the remnant will be dried up. Thus the Church, flooded with the light of the Lord, puts forth her rays through the whole world, with yet one light, which is spread upon all places, while its unity of body is not infringed. She stretches forth her branches over the universal earth, in the riches of plenty, and pours abroad her bountiful and onward streams; yet is there one head, one source, one Mother, abundant in the results of her fruitfulness.

5. It is of her womb that we are born; our nourishing is from her milk, our quickening from her breath. The spouse of Christ cannot become adulterate, she is undefiled and chaste; owning but one home, and guarding with virtuous modesty the sanctity of one chamber. She it is who keeps us for God, and appoints unto the kingdom the sons she has borne. Whosoever parts company with the Church, and joins himself to an adultress, is estranged from the promises of the Church. He who leaves the Church of Christ, attains not Christ's rewards. He is an alien, an outcast, an enemy. He can no longer have God for a Father, who has not the Church for a Mother. If any man was able to escape, who remained without the ark of Noah, then will that man escape who is out of doors beyond the Church. The Lord warns us, and says, *He who is not with Me is against Me, and he who gathereth not with Me, scattereth.* He who breaks the peace and concord of Christ, sets himself against Christ. He who gathers elsewhere but in the Church, scatters the

Church of Christ. The Lord saith, *I and the Father are one*; and again of the Father, the Son, and the Holy Ghost, it is written, *and these three are one:* and does any think, that oneness, thus proceeding from the divine immutability, and cohering in heavenly sacraments, admits of being sundered in the Church, and split by the divorce of antagonist wills? He who holds not this unity, holds not the law of God, holds not the faith of Father and Son, holds not the truth unto salvation.

6. This sacrament of unity, this bond of concord inseparably cohering, is signified in the place in the Gospel, where the coat of our Lord Jesus Christ is in no-wise parted nor cut, but is received a whole garment, by them who cast lots who should rather wear it, and is posessed as an inviolate and individual robe. The divine Scripture thus speaks, *But for the coat because it was not sewed, but woven from the top throughout, they said one to another, Let us not rend it, but cast lots whose it shall be.* It has with it a unity descending from above, as coming, that is, from heaven and from the Father; which it was not for the receiver and owner in any wise to sunder, but which he received once for all and indivisibly as one unbroken whole. He cannot own Christ's garment who splits and divides Christ's Church. On the other hand, when, on Solomon's death, his kingdom and people were split in parts, Abijah the Prophet, meeting king Jeroboam in the field, rent his garment into twelve pieces, saying, *Take thee ten pieces, for thus saith the Lord, Behold, I will rend the kingdom out of the hand of Solomom, and will give*

ten tribes unto thee; and two tribes shall be to him, for my ser-
vant David's sake, and for Jerusalem, the city which I have
chosen to place My Name there. When the twelve tribes of
Israel were torn asunder, the Prophet Abijah rent his garment. But because Christ's people cannot be rent, His coat,
woven and conjoined throughout, was not divided by those
it fell to. Individual, conjoined, coentwined, it shews the
coherent concord of our people who put on Christ. In the
sacrament and sign of His garment, He has declared the
unity of his Church.

7. Who then is the criminal and traitor, who so inflamed
by the madness of discord, as to think aught can rend, or
to venture on rending, God's unity, the Lord's garment,
Christ's Church? He Himself warns us in His Gospel,
and teaches, saying, *And there shall be one flock, and one*
Shepherd. And does any think that there can in one place
be either many shepherds, or many flocks? The Apostle
Paul likewise, intimating the same unity, solemnly exhorts,
I beseech you, brethren, by the Name of our Lord Jesus Christ,
that ye all speak the same thing, and that there be no schisms
among you; but that ye be joined together in the same mind, and
and in the same judgment. And again he says, *Forbearing*
one another in love; endeavoring to keep the unity of the Spirit
in the bond of peace. Think you that any can stand and
live, who withdraws from the Church and forms himself a
new home, and a different dwelling? Whereas it was said
to Rahab, in whom was prefigured the Church, *Thy father,*
and thy mother, and thy brethren, and all the house of thy

father, thou shalt gather unto thee into thine house ; and it shall come to pass, whosoever shall go abroad beyond the door of thine house, his blood shall be on his own head. And likewise the sacrament of the Passover doth require just this in the law of Exodus, that the lamb which is slain for a figure of Christ, should be eaten in one house. God speaks and says, *In one house shall ye eat it : ye shall not send its flesh abroad from the house.* The Flesh of Christ, and the Holy Thing of the Lord, cannot be sent abroad ; and believers have not any dwelling but the Church only. This dwelling, this hostelry of unanimity, the Holy Spirit designs and betokens in the Psalms, thus saying, *God who maketh men to dwell with one mind in an house.* In the house of God, in the Church of Christ, men dwell with one mind, in concord and singleness enduring.

8. For this cause the Holy Spirit came in the form of a dove: a simple and pleasant creature, with no bitterness of gall, no fierceness of bite, no violence of rending talons : loving the houses of men, consorting within one home, each pair nurturing their young together, when they fly abroad hanging side by side upon the wing, leading their life in mutual intercourse, giving with the bill the kiss of peace in agreement, and fulfiling a law of unanimity, in every way. This singleness of heart must be found, this habit of love be attained to in the Church; brotherly affection must make doves its pattern, gentleness and kindness must emulate lambs and sheep. What doth the savageness of wolves, in a Christian breast? or the fierceness of dogs, or the deadly

poison of serpents, or the cruel fury of wild beasts? We must be thankful when such become separate from the Church, that so their fierce and poisoned contagion may not cause a havoc among the doves and sheep of Christ ; there cannot be fellowship and union of bitter with sweet, darkness with light, foul weather with fair, war with peace, famine with plenty, drought with fountains, or storm with calm.

9. Let no one think that they can be good men, who leave the Church. Wind does not take the wheat, nor do storms overthrow the tree that has a solid root to rest on. It is the light straw that the tempest tosses, it is trees emptied of their strength that the blow of the whirlwind strike down. These the Apostle John curses and smites, saying, *They went forth from us ; but they were not of us; for if they had been of us surely they would have remained with us.* Thus is it that heresies both often have been caused, and still continue ; while the perverted mind is estranged from peace, and unity is lost amongst the faithless discord. Nevertheless, the Lord permits and suffers these things to be, preserving the power of choice to individual free-will, in order that while the discrimination of truth is a test of our hearts and minds, the perfect faith of them that are approved may shine forth in the manifest light. The Holy Spirit admonishes us by the Apostle and says, *It is needful also that heresies should be, that they which are approved may be made manifest among you.* Thus are the faithful approved, thus the false detected ; thus even here, before the day of

judgment, the souls of the righteous and unrighteous are divided, the chaff separated from the wheat.

10. These are they who, with no appointment from God, take upon them of their own will to preside over the presumptuous persons they have brought together, establish themselves as rulers without any lawful rite or ordination, and assume the name of Bishop, though no man gives them a Bishopric. These the Holy Spirit in the Psalms describes, as *sitting in the seat of pestilence*, a plague and infection of the faith, deceiving with the mouth of a serpent, cunning to corrupt truth, vomiting out deadly poisons from pestilential tongues. Whose words *spread as doth a canker :* whose writings pour a deadly poison into men's breast and hearts. Against such the Lord cries out ; from these he curbs and recalls His straying people, saying, *Hearken not unto the words of the Prophets which prophesy falsely, for the vision of their heart maketh them vain. They speak, but not out of the mouth of the Lord; they say to those who cast away the word of God, Ye shall have peace; and every one that walketh after the imagination of his own heart, no evil shall come upon him. I have not spoken to them, yet they prophesied ; if they had stood in my substance and heard My words, and taught My people, I would have turned them from their evil thoughts.* These same persons the Lord designs and signifies, saying, *They have forsaken Me, the fountain of living water, and hewed them out broken cisterns, that can hold no water.* While there can be no Baptism save one only, they think that they can baptize. They forsake the fountain of

life, yet promise the gift of a vital and saving water. **Men**
are not cleansed by them, but rather made foul; nor their
sins purged away, but even heaped up: it is a birth that
gives children not to God, but to the Devil. Born by a lie,
they cannot receive the promises of truth. Gendered of
misbelief, they lose the grace of faith. They cannot come
to the reward of peace, because they have destroyed the
peace of the Lord, in reckless discord.

11. Neither let certain persons beguile themselves by a
vain interpretation, in that the Lord hath said, *Wheresoever*
two or three are gathered together in My Name, I am with
them. Those who corrupt and falsely interpret the Gospel,
lay down what follows, but omit what goes before; giving
heed to part, while part they deceitfully suppress; as themselves are sundered from the Church, so they divide the
purport of what is one passage. For when the Lord was
impressing agreement and peace upon His Disciples, He
said, *I say unto you, that if two of you shall agree on earth,*
touching any thing that he shall ask, it shall be given you by
My Father which is in heaven. For wheresoever two or three
shall be gathered together in My Name, I am with them.
Shewing that most is given, not to the many in number
when they pray, but to oneness of heart. *If,* He saith, *two*
of you shall agree together on earth; He places agreement
first; hearts at peace are the first condition; He teaches
that we must agree together faithfully and firmly. Yet how
can he be said to be at agreement with other, who is at dis-
agreement with the body of the Church itself, and with the

universal brotherhood? How can two or three be gathered
together in Christ's name, who are manifestly separate from
Christ and from His Gospel? We did not go out from
them, but they went out from us. And whereas heresies
and schisms have a later rise, from men's setting up separate
meetings for worship, they have left the fountain head and
origin of truth. But it is of His Church, that the Lord is
speaking; and in respect of those who are in His Church,
He says, that if they are of one mind, if according to what
he bade and admonished, two or three though they be, they
gather together with agreement of the heart ; then (though
but two or three) they will be able to obtain from the
majesty of God the things which they asked for. *Wherever
two or three are gathered together in My Name I*, saith He,
am with them: that is with the single-hearted, and them
that live in peace, fearing God and keeping his commandments. With these though they be two or three, He has
said that He is. So was He with the Three Children in the
fiery furnace : and because they continued in singleness of
heart toward God, and at unity with themselves, He re-
freshed them in the midst of the encircling flames with
the breath of dew. So too was He present when the two
Apostles who were shut in prison, because they continued in
singleness and agreement of heart ; and undoing the prison-
bolts, He placed them again in the market-place, that they
might deliver to the multitude that Word which they were
faithfully preaching. When therefore He sets it forth in
His commandment, and says, *Where two or three are*

gathered together in My Name, I am with them, He does not divide men from the Church, Himself the institutor and maker of it, but rebuking the faithless for their discord, and by His voice commending peace to the faithful, He shews that He is more present with two or three which pray with one heart, than with many persons disunited from one another ; and that more can be obtained by the agreeing prayer of a few persons, than from the petitioning of many where discord is amongst them. For this cause when He gave the rule of prayer, He added, *When ye stand praying, forgive if ye have ought against any, that your Father also which is in heaven may forgive you your tresspasses;* and one who comes to the Sacrifice with a quarrel He calls back from the altar, and commands Him first to *be reconciled* with his brother, and then, when he is at peace, to return, and *offer* his *gift* to God ; for neither had God respect unto Cain's offering ; for he could not have God at peace with him, who through envy and discord was not at peace with his brother.

12. Of what peace then are they to assure themselves, who are at enmity with the brethren? What Sacrifice do they believe they celebrate, who are rivals of the Priests? Think they Christ is still in the midst of them when gathered together, though gathered beyond Christ's Church? If such men were even killed for confession of the Christian Name, not even by their blood is this stain washed out. Inexpiable and heavy is the sin of discord, and is purged by no suffering. He cannot be a Martyr, who is not in the

Church; he can never attain to the kingdom, who leaves
her, with whom the kingdom shall be. Christ gave us
peace; He bade us be of one heart and one mind; He commanded that the covenant of affection and charity should
be kept unbroken and inviolate; he cannot shew himself as
a Martyr, who has not kept the love of the brotherhood.
The Apostle Paul teaches this, thus witnessing; *And though
I have faith, so that I can remove mountains, and have not
charity, I am nothing : and though I give all my goods to feed
the poor, and though I give my body to be burned, and have not
charity, it profiteth me nothing. Charity suffereth long and is
kind; charity envieth not, charity acteth not vainly, is not puffed
up, is not easily provoked, thinketh no evil; is pleased with all
things, believeth all things, hopeth all things, endureth all things;
charity never faileth. Charity*, he saith, *never faileth ;* for
she will reign for ever, she will abide evermore in the unity
of a brotherhood which entwines itself around her. In the
kingdom of heaven discord cannot enter; it cannot gain the
reward of Christ who said, *This is My commandment, that ye
love one another, as I have loved you.* It will never be his to
belong to Christ, who has violated the love of Christ by unfaithful dissension. He who has not love, has not God. It
is the word of the blessed Apostle John, *God*, saith he, *is
love; and he that dwelleth in love, dwelleth in God, and God in
him.* They cannot dwell with God, who have refused to be
of one mind in God's Church; though they be given over
to be burnt in flame and fire, or yield their lives a prey to
wild beasts, theirs will not be the crown of faith, but the

penalty of unfaithfulness ; not the glorious issue of dutiful valour, but the death of despair. A man of such sort may indeed be killed, crowned he cannot be.

13. He professes himself a christian after the manner in which the Devil oftentimes feigns himself to be Christ, as the Lord himself forwarns us, saying, *Many shall come in my Name, saying, I am Christ, and shall deceive many.* No more than he is Christ, though he deceive beneath His Name, can he be looked upon as a Christian, who does not abide in the truth of His Gospel and of faith. To prophesy, to cast out devils, to perform great miracles on earth, is a high, doubtless, and a wonderful thing ; yet the man who is found in all these things attains not to the heavenly kingdom, unless he walk in an observance of the straight and righteous way. The Lord speaks this denunciation ; *Many shall say to Me in that day, Lord, Lord, have we not prophesied in Thy Name done many wonderful works ? And then will I profess unto them, I never knew you ; depart from Me, ye that work iniquity.* Righteousness is the thing needful, before any one can find grace with God the Judge. We must obey his instructions and warnings, in order that our deserts may receive their reward. When the Lord in the Gospel would direct the path of our hope and faith in a summary of words ; *The Lord thy God,* He saith, *is one : and thou shall love the Lord thy God with all thy heart, and with all thy soul, and with all thy strength. This is the first commandment ; and the second is like unto it ; Thou shall love thy neighbour as thyself. On these two commandments hangs all the Laws and*

the Prophets. Unity and love together is the instruction which He teaches us ; in two commandments He has included all the Prophets and the Law. Yet what unity does he keep, what love does he either maintain, or have a thought for, who, maddened by the heat of discord, rends the Church, pulls down faith, troubles peace, scatters charity, profanes the sacrament ?

14. This mischief, dearest brethren, had long before begun, but in these days the dire havoc of this same evil has been gaining growth, and the envenomed pest of heretical perverseness and of schisms is shooting up and sprouting afresh ; for thus must it be in the end of the world, the Holy Spirit having forespoken by the Apostle, and forewarned us. *In the last days,* saith He, *perilous times shall come, for men shall be lovers of their own selves, proud, boasters, covetous, blasphemers, disobedient to parents, unthankful, unholy, without natural affection, trucebreakers, false accusers, incontinent, fierce, despisers of the good, traitors, heady, high minded, lovers of pleasures more than lovers of God, having a form of godliness, but denying the power thereof. Of this sort are they which creep into houses, and lead captive silly women laden with sins, led away with divers lusts ; ever learning, and never coming to the knowledge of the truth. Now as Jamnes and Mambres withstood Moses, so do these also resist the truth ; men of corrupt minds, reprobate concerning the faith ; but they shall proceed no further, for their folly shall be manifest unto all men, as theirs also was.* Whatever things were predicted, are in fulfilment ; and, as the end of time draws nigh, they

have come to us in trial both of men and times. As the
adversary rages more and more, error deceives, haughtiness
lifts aloft, envy inflames, covetousness blinds, unholiness
depraves, pride puffs up, quarrels embitter, and anger
hurries men headlong. Let not however the extreme and
headlong faithlessness of many move and disturb us, but
rather let it give support to our faith, as the event was declared to us beforehand. As some have become such, because this was foretold beforehand, so (because this too was
foretold beforehand) let the other brethren take heed against
them, according as the Lord instructs us and says, *But take
ye heed; behold, I have told you all things.* Do ye avoid such
men, I beseech you, and put away from beside you, and
from your hearing, their pernicious converse, as though a
deadly contagion; as it is written, *Hedge thine ears about
with thorns and refuse to hear a wicked tongue.* And again,
Evil communications corrupt good manners. The Lord
teaches and warns us, that we must withdraw ourselves
from such. *They be blind,* saith He, *leaders of the blind; and
if the blind lead the blind, both shall fall into the ditch.* Whosoever is separated from the Church, such a man is to be
avoided and fled from. *Such an one is subverted and sinneth,
being condemned of himself.* Thinks he that he is with
Christ, who does counter to the Priests of Christ? who
separates himself from the fellowship of His clergy and
people? That man bears arms against the Church, he with-
stands God's appointment ; an enemy to the altar, a rebel
against the Sacrifice of Christ, for faith perfidious, for

religion sacrilegious, a servant not obedient, a son not pious, a brother not loving, setting Bishops at nought, and deserting the Priests of God, he dares to build another altar, to offer another prayer with unlicensed words, to profane by false sacrifices the truth of the Lord's Sacrifice. He is not permitted to a knowledge of what he does, since he who strives against the appointment of God, is punished by the divine censure, for the boldness of his daring.

15. Thus Korah, Dathan, and Abiram, who endeavoured to maintain to themselves the privilege of sacrificing, in opposition to Moses and Aaron the Priest, forthwith paid penalty for their attempts. The earth burst its fastenings, and opened the depth of its bosom ; standing and alive, the guilt of the parting ground swallowed them. Nor those only who had been movers, did the wrath of an angered God strike ; but the two hundred and fifty besides, partakers and companions of the same madness, who had mixed with them in their bold work, a fire going out from the Lord with speedy vengeance consumed ; warning and manifesting, that that is done against God, whatsoever evil men of human will endeavour, for the pulling down of God's ordinance. Thus also Uzziah the king who bare the censer, and contrary to God's law, did by violence take to himself to sacrifice, refusing to be obedient and to give way when Azariah the Priest withstood him, he being confounded by the wrath of God, was polluted by the spot of leprosy upon his forehead ; in that part of his body was marked by his offended Lord, where they are marked, who have the grace

of the Lord assigned them. The sons of Aaron also who put strange fire upon the altar, which the Lord had not commanded, were speedily consumed in the presence of their avenging Lord. All such are imitated and followed by them, who, despising God's tradition, lust for strange doctrines, and give inlet to ordinances of human imposition; these the Lord rebukes and reproves in His Gospel, thus saying, *Ye reject the commandment of God, that ye may establish your own tradition.*

16. This crime is worse, than that which the lapsed appear to commit ; who, at least, when in the condition of penitents for their offence, seek their peace with God, by full satisfactions. In this case the Church is enquired after and applied to; in the other the Church is resisted : here there may have been compulsion in guilt; there free choice is involved : the lapsed harms only himself, but one who undertakes to raise heresy and schism, is a deceiver of many, by leading them along with him. The one both understands that he has sinned, and laments and mourns it ; the other, puffed up in its wickedness, and finding pleasure in his own offences, separates sons from the Mother, entices sheep from their shepherd, and disturbs the Sacraments of God. And whereas the lapsed has committed one offence, the other is an offender every day : lastly, the lapsed, if he be admitted to martyrdom afterwards, may reap the promises of the kingdom ; the other, if he be killed out of the Church, cannot attain to the Church's rewards.

17. Neither let any one wonder, dearest brethren, that

some, even from among Confessors, adventure thus far: that even from among them there are those who sin thus greatly, and thus grievously. Confession does not make a man safe from the crafts of the Devil, nor, while he is still placed in this world, encompass him with perpetual security against its temptations, and dangers, and assaults, and shocks; were it so, we should never witness in Confessors those after commissions of fraud, fornication, and adultery, which we now groan and grieve at seeing in some of them. Whosoever any Confessor may be, he is not a greater man than Solomon, nor a better, nor one more dear to God: who, nevertheless, so long as he walked in the ways of the Lord, continued to be gifted with that grace which from the Lord he obtained; but when he deserted the way of the Lord, he lost the Lord's grace; as it is written, *And the Lord raised up the Adversary against Solomon.* It is for this cause written, *Hold that fast which thou hast, that no man take thy crown.* This the Lord would not threaten, that the crown of righteousness can be taken away, except because when righteousness goes from us, the crown must go from us also. Confession is the beginning of glory, not the full price of the crown ; it is not the perfection of our praise, but the entrance upon our honour : and whereas it is written, *He that endureth to the end shall be saved,* all that is before the end, is the stepping whereby one mounts toward the height of salvation, not the close at where the full summit is gained. If any is a Confessor, then his danger is the greater after confession, because the Adversary is more

provoked ; if he is a Confessor, he ought the more truly to
stand with the Gospel of the Lord, since through the Gospel
he has gained his glory from the Lord : for the Lord says,
*To whom much is given, of him shall much be required; and to
whom more dignity is ascribed, of him more service is exacted.*
Let none ever perish through a Confessor's example ; let
none learn injustice, insolence, or misbelief, from the manners of a Confessor. If he is a Confessor, let him be humble
and quiet ; let him exercise in his conduct the modesty of a
disciplined state, and being called a Confessor of Christ, let
him imitate Christ whom he confesses. For since He says,
*Whosoever shall exalt himself shall be abased, and he that shall
humble himself shall be exalted;* and since Himself has been
exalted by the Father, because being the Word, and Power,
and Wisdom of God the Father, He humbled Himself upon
earth, how can He love exaltation, having both commanded
humility from us by His law, and Himself received from the
Father a most excellent Name, as a reward of His humilia-
tion ? If any is a Confessor of Christ, he is such no more, if
the majesty and dignity of Christ is afterwards blasphemed
through him. The tongue that has confessed Christ, must
not speak evil only, not be clamorous, not be heard dinning
with reproaches and quarrels, nor, after words of worship,
dart serpent's poison against the Brethern and Priests of
God. But if a man afterwards becomes guilty and hateful,
if he is wasteful of his confession by an evil conversation,
and blots his life by a vile unholiness ; if, in fine, deserting
that Church in which he had become a Confessor, and rend-

ing the concord of unity, he transforms what was faith before, into faithlessness afterwards, he must not flatter himself on the score of his Confession, that he is one elected to the reward of Glory, since the desert of punishment is rendered greater on this ground ; for the Lord chose Judas among the Apostles, and yet Judas afterwards betrayed the Lord.

18. The faith and firmness of the Apostles did not thereupon fail, because the traitor Judas was a deserter from their fellowship; and thus neither here is the sanctity and dignity of Confessors forthwith impaired, because the faith of certain of them is broken. The blessed Apostle in his Epistle thus speaks; *For what if some did not believe? shall their unbelief make the faith of God without effect? God forbid: yea, let God be true, but every man a liar.* The larger and better part of the Confessors stands in the strength of their faith, and in the truth of the law and discipline of the Lord. Neither do they depart from the peace of the Church, who bear in mind that in the Church they gained grace from God's bounty; but hereby they reach a higher praise of faith, because that separating from the faithlessness of persons, who were fellows with them in Confession, they withdrew from the contagion of guilt; and illuminated by the true light of the Gospel, overshone with pure and white brightness of the Lord, they have praise in keeping Christ's peace, not less than their victory, in combating the Devil.

19. It is my desire, dearest brethren, it is the end both of my endeavours and exhortations, that, if it be possible,

no one of the Brethren may perish, but our rejoicing Mother may fold within her bosom the one body of a people agreeing together: but if saving counsel cannot recal to the way of salvation certain leaders of schisms and authors of dissensions, who abide on in their blind and obstinate madness, yet do the rest of you who are either betrayed through simplicity, or drawn on by error, or deceived through some artfulness of a cunning craftiness, release yourselves from the toils of deceitfulness, free your wayward steps from their wanderings, submit to that straight path which leads to heaven! It is the word of the Apostle uttering witness; *We command you*, he says, *in the Name of our Lord Jesus Christ, that ye withdraw yourselves from every brother that walketh disorderly, and not after the tradition he hath received from us.* And again he says, *Let no man deceive you with vain words ; for because of these things cometh the wrath of God upon the children of disobedience. Be not ye therefore partakers with them.* We must withdraw from them that go astray, nay rather must flee from them, lest any joining himself with those who walk evily, and going in ways of error and guilt, should himself lose the true path, and be found in an equal guilt. There is One God, and One Christ, and His Church One, and the Faith One, and a people joined in solid oneness of body by a cementing concord. Unity cannot be sundered, nor can one body be divided by a dissolution of its structure, nor be cast peacemeal abroad with vitals torn and lacerated. Parted from the womb, nothing can live and breathe in its separated state ; it loses its principle of health. The Holy Spirit warns us and says, *What man is he that lusteth to live, and would fain see good days? Refrain thy tongue from evil, and thy lips that they speak no guile. Eschew evil and do good, seek peace and ensue it.* Peace ought the son of peace to seek and ensue ; he who understands and cherishes the bond of charity, should refrain his tongue from the evil of dissent. Amongst His divine commands and saving instructions, the Lord now nigh to passion spoke this beside ; *Peace I leave with you, My peace I give unto you.* This is the legacy which Christ has given us ; all the gifts and rewards which He foretokens to us, He promises to the preserving of peace. If we are Christ's heirs, let us abide in the peace of Christ ; if we are sons of God we ought to be peacemakers; *Blessed*, He says, *are the peacemakers, for they shall be called the sons of God.* The sons of God ought to be peacemakers, mild in heart, simple in words, agreed in feelings, faithfully entwining one with another by links of unanimity. Under the Apostles of old there was this oneness of mind ; it was thus that the new congregation of·believers, keeping the commandments of the Lord, preserved its charity. Divine Scripture proves it, which says, *The multitude of them that believed were of one heart and of one soul :* and again ; *These all continued with one mind in prayer with the women, and Mary the Mother of Jesus, and with His brethren.* Therefore they prayed with effectual prayers, and were with confidence enabled to obtain whatsoever they required of the Lord's mercy.

20. But in us unanimity has as greatly fallen away, as has bountifulness in works of charity decayed. Then they gave houses and lands for sale, and laying up for themselves treasures in heaven, offered the price to the Apostles to be distributed for the uses of the needy. But now we give not even the tithes from our property, and while the Lord bids us to sell, we rather buy and heap up. It is thus that the vigour of our faith has waxed faint, and the strength of the believers has languished; and hence the Lord, looking to our times, says in His Gospel, *When the Son of Man cometh, shall He find faith on the earth?* We see come to pass that which He foretold. In the fear of God, in the law of righteousness, in love, in good works, our faith is nought. No man from fear of things to come, gives heed to the day of the Lord and the anger of God ; none considers the punishments which will come on the unbelieving, and the eternal torments to the faithless. What our conscience would fear if it believed, that, because nowise believing, it fear not : if it believed, it would take heed ; if it took heed, it would escape. Let us awaken ourselves, dearest brethren, what we can, and breaking off the slumbers of our slothfulness, let us be watching, for observance and fulfilment of the Lord's commands. Let us be such as He bade us be when He said, *Let your loins be girded about, and your lamps burning, and ye yourselves like unto to men that wait for their Lord, when He will return from the wedding, that when He cometh and knocketh, they may open unto Him : blessed are those servants, whom their Lord, when He cometh shall find*

watching. We need not be girded about, lest when the day
of march cometh, He find us hindered and impeded. Let
our light shine in good works, let it so beam forth, as to be
our guide out of this night below, into the brightness of
eternal day. Let us ever in anxiety and cautiousness be
awaiting the sudden advent of the Lord, that when He
knocketh our faith may be on the watch, and gain from the
Lord the reward of its watchfulness. If these commandments be observed, if these warnings and precepts are kept,
we can never be overtaken in slumber by the deceit of the
Devil, but shall reign, as servants who watch, in the kingdom of Christ.

II.

ST. CYRIL.

CATECHETICAL LECTURE 18.

" The Faith which we rehearse contains in order the following, ' And in one Baptism of repentance for the remission of sin ; and in one Holy Catholic Church ; and in the
resurrection of the flesh ; and in eternal life.' Now of
Baptism and repentance I have spoken in the foregoing
Lectures ; and my present remarks concerning the resurrection of the dead have been made with reference to the
Article, ' In the resurrection of the flesh.' Now then let me
finish what remains to be said, in consequence of the Article,

'In one Holy Catholic Church,' on which, though one
might say many things, we will speak but briefly.

Now it is called Catholic because it is throughout the
world, from one end of the earth to the other ; and because
it teaches universally and completely one and all the
doctrines which ought to come to men's knowledge, concerning things both visible and invisible, heavenly and earthly ;
and because it subjugates in order to godliness every class
of men, governors and governed, learned and unlearned ;
and because it universally treats and heals every sort of sins,
which are committed by soul or body, and possesses in itself
every form of virtue which is named, both in deeds and
words, and in every kind of spiritual gifts.

And it is rightly named Church, because it calls forth and
assembles together all men ; according as the Lord says in
Leviticus, *And assemble thou all the congregation to the doors
of the tabernacle of witness.* And it is to be noted, that the
word *assemble*, is used for the first time in the Scriptures
here, at the time when the Lord puts Aaron into the High-
priesthood. And in Deuteronomy the Lord says to Moses,
*Assemble to Me the people, and I will make them hear My
words, that they shall learn to fear me.* And he again men-
tions the name of the Church, when he says concerning the
Tables, *And on them was written according to all the words which
the Lord spake with you in the mount of the midst of the fire in
the day of the Assembly;* as if he had said more plainly, in the
day in which ye were called and gathered together by God.
And the Psalmist says, *I will give Thee thanks in the great
Assembly; I will praise Thee among much people.*

Of old the Psalmist sung, *Bless ye God in the Church, even the Lord, from the fountain of Israel.* But since the Jews for their evil designs against the Saviour have been cast away from grace, the Saviour has built out of the Gentiles a second Holy Church, the Church of us Christians, concerning which He said to Peter, *And upon this rock I will build My Church, and the gates of hell shall not prevail against it.* And David prophesying of both, said plainly of the first which was rejected, *I have hated the Church of the evil doers;* but of the second which is built up he says in the same Psalm, *Lord, I have loved the habitation of Thine house;* and immediately afterwards, *In the Churches will I bless the Lord;* For now that the one Church in Judæa is cast off, the Churches of Christ are increased throughout the world ; and of them it is said, *Sing unto the Lord a new song, and His praise in the Church of the Saints.* Agreeably to which the Prophet also said to the Jews, *I have no pleasure in you saith the Lord of Hosts;* and immediately afterwards, *For from the rising of the sun even unto the going down of the same, My name shall be great among the Gentiles.* Concerning this Holy Catholic Church Paul writes to Timothy, *That thou mayest know how thou oughtest to behave thyself in the house of God, which is the Church of the living God, the pillar and ground of the truth.*

But since the word Church or Assembly is applied to different things, (as also it is written of the multitude in the theatre of the Ephesians, *And when he had thus spoken, he dismissed the Assembly*, and since one might properly and truly say that there is a *Church of the evil doers*, I mean the meeting of the heretics, the Marcionists and Manichees, and the rest) the Faith has delivered to thee by way of security the Article, ' And in One Holy Catholic Church ; ' that thou mayest avoid their wretched meetings, and ever abide with the Holy Church Catholic in which thou wast regenerated. And if ever thou art sojourning in any city, inquire not simply where the Lord's House is, (for the sects of the profane also make an attempt to call their own dens, houses of the Lord), nor merely where the Church is, but where is the Catholic Church. For this is the peculiar name of this Holy Body, the mother of us all, which is the spouse of our Lord Jesus Christ, the Only-begotten Son of God, (for it is written, *As Christ also loved the Church, and gave Himself for it*, and all the rest), and is a figure and copy of Jerusalem *above, which is free, and the mother of us all;* which before barren, but now has many children.

For when the first Church was cast off, God, in the second, which is the Catholic Church, *hath set first Apostles, secondarily Prophets, thirdly teachers, after that miracles, then gifts of healings, helps, governments, diversities of tongues*, and every sort of virtue ; I mean wisdom and understanding, temperance and justice, alms-doing and loving-kindness, and patience unconquerable in persecutions. She, *by the armour of righteousness on the right hand and on the left, by honour and dishonour*, in former days amid persecutions and tribulations crowned the holy martyrs with the varied and blooming chaplets of patience, and now in times of peace by God's grace receives her due honours from princes and nobles, and from every rank and kindred of man. And while the kings of particular nations have bounds set to their dominion, the Holy Church Catholic alone extends her illimitable sovereignty over the whole world ; *for God*, as it is written, *hath made her border peace*. But I should need many more hours for my discourse, would I speak of all things which concern her.

In this Holy Catholic Church receiving instruction and behaving ourselves virtuously, we shall attain the kingdom of heaven, and inherit eternal life ; for which also we endure all toils, that we may be made partakers of it from the Lord. For ours is no trifling aim ; eternal life is our object of pursuit."

III.

ST. PACIAN.

ON THE CATHOLIC NAME.

Pacian to Sympronian his brother, greeting.

1. If it be not a carnal intention, my lord, but as I judge, a calling of the Spirit, that thou enquirest of us the faith of the Catholic verity, thou, before all, taking thy rise as far as appears; from a streamlet at a distance, and not holding to the fountain and source of the principal Church, shouldest, in the first instance, have shewn what or how different are

the opinions which thou followest. Thou shouldest unfold thyself as to what cause more particularly had loosened thee from the unity of our body. For those parts, for which a remedy is sought, should be laid bare. Whereas now (if I may so say) the bosom of correspondence being closed, we see not on what members more especially we have to bestow our care. For such are the heresies which have sprung forth from the Christian head, that of the mere names the roll would be immense. For to pass over the heretics of the Jews, Dositheus the Samaratan, the Sadducees, and the Pharisees, it were long to enumerate how many grew up in the times of the Apostles, Simon Magus, and Menander, and Nicolaus, and others hidden by an inglorious fame. What again in later times were Ebion, and Apelles, and Marcion, and Valentinus, and Cerdon, and not long after them, the Cataphrygians, and Novatians, not to notice any recent swarms!

2. Whom then in my letters must I first refute? Wouldest thou the mere names of all, my paper will not contain them; unless indeed by your writings every way condemnatory of penance you declare your agreement with the Phrygians. But, most illustrious Lord, so manifold and so diverse is the error of these very men, that in them we have not only to overthrow their peculiar fancies against penance but to cut off the heads, as it were, of some Lernæan monster. And, in the first place, they rely on more founders than one, for I suppose Blastus the Greek is of them; Theodotus also and Praxeas were once teachers of your

party, themselves also Phrygians of some celebrity, who falsely say they are inspired of Leucius, boast that they are instructed by Proculus. Following Montanus, and Maximilla, and Priscilla, how manifold controversies have they raised concerning the day of Easter, the Paraclete, Apostles, Prophets, and many other disputes, as this also concerning the Catholic name, the pardon of penance.

3. Wherefore if we would discuss all these points, thou hadst need been present and teachable. But if on those points merely on which thou writest, my instruction should not be sufficiently full, yet as it is our duty to serve, in whatsoever way we can, those who solemnly adjure us, we now, for the sake of informing you, discourse with thee summarily, on those matters about which thou hast deigned to write to us. If thou wouldest have fuller knowledge on our side, thou must on thine declare thyself more unreservedly, lest by somewhat of obscurity in thy enquiries, thou leave us uncertain, whether thou art consulting or censuring.

4. Meanwhile (and this concerns our present correspondence) I would above all entreat thee not to borrow authority for error from this very fact that, as thou sayest, throughout the whole world no one has been found, who could convince or persuade thee contrary to what thou believest. For although we be unskilled, most skilful is the Spirit of God, and if we are faithless, *faithful is God, Who cannot deny Himself.* Then, also, because it was not allowed the Priests of God to contend long with one who resisted. *We,* says the Apostle, *have no such custom, neither the*

churches, of God. After one admonition, as thou thyself knowest, *the contentious is passed by.* For who can persuade any of anything against his will? Thine own fault was it therefore, brother, and not theirs, if no one convinced thee of what in itself is most excellent. For at this day too it is in thy power to despise our writings also, if thy hadst rather refute than approve them. Yet very many resisted both the Lord Himself, and the Apostles, nor could any ever be persuaded of the truth, unless he consented to it by his own religious feeling.

5. Therefore, my Lord, neither have we written with that confidence as though we could persuade thee, if thou resistest, but in that faith by which we would not deny thee an entrance to wholly peace, if thou willest. Which peace if it be after thine own soul and heart, there ought to be no contest about the name of Catholic. For if it is through God that our people obtain this name, no question is to be raised, when Divine authority is followed. If through man, you must discover when it was first taken. Then, if the name is good, no odium rests with it; if ill, it need not be envied. The Novatians, I hear, are called after Novatus or Novatian ; yet it is the sect which I accuse in them, not the name : nor has any one objected their name to Montanus or the Phrygians

6. But under the Apostles, you will say, no one was called Catholic. Be it thus. It shall have been so. Allow even that. When after the Apostles heresies had burst forth, and were striving under various names to tear piece-

meal and divide *the Dove* and *the Queen* of God, did not the Apostolic people require a name of their own, whereby to mark the unity of the people that were uncorrupted, lest the error of some should rend limb by limb the *undefiled virgin* of God? Was it not seemly that the chief head should be distinguished by its own peculiar appellation? Suppose, this very day, I entered a populous city. When I had found Marcionites, Apollinarians, Cataphrygians, Novatians, and others of the kind who call themselves Christians, by what name should I recognize the congregation of my own people, unless it were named Catholic? Come tell me, who bestowed so many names on the other peoples? Why have so many cities, so many nations, each their own description? The man who asks the meaning of the Catholic Name, will he be ignorant himself of the cause of his own name if I shall enquire its origin? Whence was it delivered to me? Certainly that which has stood through so many ages was not borrowed from man. This name "Catholic" sounds not of Marcion, nor Apelles, nor of Montanus, nor does it take heretics as its authors.

7. Many things the Holy Spirit hath taught us, Whom God sent from Heaven to the Apostles as their Comforter and Guide. Many things reason teaches us, as Paul saith, and honesty, and, as he says, *nature herself*. What! is the authority of Apostolic men, of Primitive Priests, of the most blessed Martyr and Dr. Cyprian, of slight weight with us? Do we wish to teach the teacher? Are we wiser than he was, and are we puffed up by the spirit of the flesh

against the man, whom his noble shedding of blood, and a crown of most glorious suffering, have set forth as a witness of the Eternal God ? What thinkest thou of so many Priests on the same side, who throughout the whole world were compacted together in one bond of peace with this same Cyprian ? What of so many aged Bishops, so many Martyrs, so many Confessors ? Come say, if they were not sufficient authorities for the use of this name, are we sufficient for its rejection ? And shall the Fathers rather follow our authority, and the antiquity of Saints give way to be emended by us, and times now putrifying through their sins, pluck out the grey hairs of Apostolic age? And yet, my brother, be not troubled; Christian is my name, but Catholic my surname. The former gives me a name, the latter distinguishes me. By the one I am approved ; by the other I am but marked.

8. And if at last we must give an account of the word Catholic, and draw it out from the Greek by a Latin interpretation, " Catholic " is ' every where one,' or (as learned men think,) " obedience in all, i. e. all the commands of God. Whence the Apostle, *Whether ye be obedient in all things :* and again, *For as by one man's disobedience many were made sinners, so by the obedience of One shall many be made righteous.* Therefore he who is a Catholic, the same man is obedient. He who is obedient, the same is a Christian, and thus the Catholic is a Christian. Wherefore our people when named Catholic are separated by this appellation from the heretical name. But if also the word

Catholic means 'every where one,' as those first think, David indicates this very thing, when he saith, *The queen did stand in a vesture of gold, wrought about with divers colours:* that is, one amidst all. And in the Song of Songs the Bridegroom speaketh these words, *My dove, My unde-filed is but one; she is the only one of her mother; she is the choice one of her that bare her.* Again it is written, *The virgins shall be brought unto the king after her.* And further, *Virgins without number.* Therefore amidst all she is one, and one over all. If thou askest the reason of the name, it is evident.

9. But as to penance, God grant that it may be necessary for none of the faithful ; that no one after the help of the sacred font may *fall into the pit* of death, and that Priests may not be compelled to inculcate or to teach its tardy con-solations lest, whilst by remedies they soothe the sinner, they open a road to sin. But we lay open this indulgence of our God to the miserable, not to the happy ; not before sin, but after sins ; nor do we announce a medicine to the whole, but to the sick. If spiritual wickednesses have no power over the baptized, none, that fraud of the serpent, which subverted the first man, which hath printed on his posterity so many marks of condemnation; if it hath retired from the world, if we have already begun to reign, if no crime steals over our eyes, none over our hands, none over our minds, then let this gift of God be cast aside, this help rejected ; be no confession, no groans, heard : let a proud righteousness despise every remedy.

10. But if the Lord Himself hath provided these things for His own creature man, if the same Lord Who hath bestowed remedies on the fallen, hath given rewards to them that stand, cease to accuse the Divine goodness, to erase by the interposition of your own rigour so many inscriptions of heavenly mercy, or by inexorable harshness to prohibit the gratuitous good gifts of the Lord. This is not a largess from our own bounty. *Turn ye*, saith the Lord, *even to Me, and with fasting, and with weeping, and with mourning : and rend your heart;* and again, *Let the wicked man leave his ways, and the unrighteous man his thoughts and turn unto the Lord, and he shall obtain mercy.* And also after this manner crieth the Prophet, *For He is gracious, and merciful, slow to anger, and of great kindness, and repenteth Him of the evil.* Hath the serpent so lasting a poison, and hath not Christ a remedy? Doth the Devil kill in the world, and hath Christ no power here to help? Be we indeed ashamed to sin, but not ashamed to repent. Be we ashamed to hazard ourselves, but not ashamed to be delivered. Who will snatch the plank from the shipwrecked, that he escape not? Who will grudge the curing of a wound? Doth not David say, *Every night I will wash my bed, I will water my couch with my tears;* and again, *I acknowledge my sin, and mine unrighteousness have I not hid;* and yet more, *I said, I will confess my sin unto the Lord, and so Thou forgavest the wickedness of my heart.* Did not the Prophet answer him when, after the guilt of murder and adultery, penitent for Bathsheba, *The Lord also hath put away from thee thy sin?*

Did not confession deliver the King of Babylon, when condemned after so many sins of Idolatry ? And what is it that
the Lord saith, *Shalt he who has fallen not arise and, and he
who has turned not return ?* What answer give the subjects
of those many parables of our Lord ? That the woman
findeth the coin, and rejoiceth when she hath found it ?
That the shepherd carrieth back the wandering sheep ?
That when the son was returning, all his goods wasted in
riotous living with harlots and fornicators, the Father with
kindness met him, and, assigning the grounds, chideth the
envious brother, saying, *This my son was dead, and is alive
again, was lost and is found.* What of him who was
wounded in the way, whom Levite and Priest passed by ?
Is he not taken care of ?

11. Ponder what the Spirit saith to the Churches. The
Ephesians He accuses of having forsaken their love; to them
of Thyatira He imputeth fornication; the people of Sardis
He blameth as loitering in the work; those of Pergamus as
teaching things contrary; of the Laodiceans He brandeth
the riches; and yet He calleth all to penance and to satis-
faction. What meaneth the Apostle, when he writeth to the
Corinthians thus, *Lest, when I bewail many which have sinned
already, and have not repented of the uncleanliness, and fornication, and lasciviousness which they have committed?* What,
when again to the Galatians, *If a man be overtaken in a fault*
(i. e. any whatever,) *ye who are spiritual restore such an one
in the spirit of meekness, considering thyself, lest thou also be
tempted.* Does then the master of the family in a large

house guard only the silver and golden vessels? Does he not deign to guard both the earthen and the wooden, and some that are put together and repaired? *Now I rejoice*, saith the Apostle, *that ye sorrowed to repentance :* and again, *for godly sorrow worketh repentance unto enduring salvation.* But penitence you say was not allowed. No one enjoins a fruitless labour; *For the labourer is worthy of his hire.* Never would God threaten the impenitent, unless He would pardon the penitent. This, you will say, God alone can do. It is true. But that also which He does through His Priests, is His own authority. Else what is that he saith to the Apostles, *Whatsoever ye shall bind on earth, shall be bound in heaven, and whatsoever ye shall loose on earth, shall be loosed in heaven?* Why said he this, if it was not lawful for men to bind and loose? Is this allowed to Apostles only? Then to them also is it allowed to baptize, and to them only to give the Holy Spirit, and to them only to cleanse the sins of the nations; for all this was enjoined on none others but Apostles.

12. But if both the loosening of bonds and the power of the Sacrament are given in one place, either the whole has been derived to us from the Apostolic form and authority, or else not even this relaxation has been made from the decree. *I*, he saith, *have laid the foundation, and another buildeth thereon.* This, therefore we build up, which the doctrine of the Apostles laid as the foundation. And, lastly, Bishops also are named Apostles, as saith Paul of Epaphroditus, *My brother and fellow-soldier but your Apostle.*

13. If, therefore the power of the Laver, and of the An-

ointing, gifts far greater, descended thence to Bishops, then the right of binding and of loosing was with them. Which although for our sins it be presumptuous in us to claim, yet God, Who hath granted unto Bishops the name even of His only Beloved, will not deny it unto them, as if holy and sitting in the chair of the Apostles.

14. I would write more brother, were I not pressed by the hasty return of the servant, and were not reserving a fuller account for thee when either present, or making confession of thy whole purport. Let no one despise the Bishop on consideration of the man. Let us remember that the Apostle Peter hath named our Lord, Bishop. *But are now*, he saith, *returned unto the Shepherd, and Bishop of your souls*. What shall be denied to the Bishop, in whom operateth the Name of God? He shall indeed give an account if he have done anything wrong, or if he shall have judged corrupt and unrighteous judgment. Nor is God's Judgment forestalled, but that He may undo the work of a wicked builder. In the mean while, if that his ministration be holy, he abideth as an helper in the work of God. See the Apostle writeth to Laity : *To whom ye forgive anything, I forgive also: for if I forgave anything, to whom I forgave it, for your sakes forgave I it in the person of Christ; lest Satan should get an advantage of us : for we are not ignorant of his devices.* But if what the Laity forgive, the Apostle saith that he hath forgiven, what a Bishop hath done, in what character can it be rejected? Therefore neither the Anointing, nor Baptism, nor remis-

sion of sins, nor the renewing of the Body, were granted to his sacred authority, because nothing was entrusted to him as assumed by himself, but the whole has descended in a stream from the Apostolic privilege.

15. Know, brother, that not indiscriminately to all is this very pardon through penance granted ; nor until there shall have been either some indication of the Divine will, or perchance some visitation, many men be *loosed;* that with careful ponderance and much balancing, after many groans and much shedding of tears, after the prayers of the whole Church, pardon is in such wise not refused to true penitence, as that no one thereby prejudgeth the future Judgment of Christ. If, brother, thou wouldest write thy sentiments more openly, thou shalt be more fully instructed.

IV.

MACAULAY.

ESSAY ON RANKE'S HISTORY OF THE POPES.

'There is not, and there never was, on earth a work of human policy so well deserving of examination as the Roman Catholic Church. The history of that Church joins together the two great ages of human civilization. No other institution is left standing which carries the mind back to the times when the smoke of sacrifice rose from the Pantheon, and when camelopards and tigers bounded in the Flavian amphitheatre. The proudest royal houses are but

of yesterday when compared with the line of the supreme
Pontiffs. That line we trace back in an unbroken series
from the Pope who crowned Napoleon in the nineteenth
century, to the Pope who crowned Pepin in the eighth ; and
far beyond 'he time of Pepin the august dynasty extends
till it is lost in the twilight of fable. The Republic of
Venice came next in antiquity. But the Republic of Venice was modern when compared to the Papacy ; and the
Republic of Venice is gone, and the Papacy remains. The
Papacy remains, not in decay, not a mere antique, but full of
life and youthful vigor. The Catholic Church is still sending
forth to the farthest ends of the world missionaries as zealous as those who landed in Kent with Augustine, and still
confronting hostile kings with the same spirit with which
she confronted Attila. The number of her children is
greater than in any former age. Her acquisitions in the
New World have more than compensated for what she has
lost in the Old. Her spiritual ascendency extends over the
vast countries which lie between the plains of the Missouri
and Cape Horn, countries which, a century hence, may not
improbably contain a population as large as that which now
inhabits Europe. The members of her communion are
certainly not fewer than a hundred and fifty millions ; and
it will be difficult to show that all other Christian sects
united amount to a hundred and twenty millions. Nor do
we see any sign which indicates that the term of her long
dominion is approaching. She saw the commencement of
all the governments and of all the ecclesiastical establish-

ments that now exist in the world ; and we feel no assurance that she is not destined to see the end of them all. She was great and respected before the Saxon had set foot on Britain, before the Frank had passed the Rhine, when Grecian eloquence still flourished at Antioch, when idols were still worshipped in the temple of Mecca. And she may still exist in undiminished vigor when some traveller from New Zealand shall, in the midst of a vast solitude, take his stand on a broken arch of London Bridge to sketch the ruins of St. Paul's.'

' We often hear it said that the world is constantly becoming more and more enlightened, and that this enlightening must be favorable to Protestantism, and unfavourable to Catholicism. We wish that we could think so. But we see great reason to doubt whether this be a well founded expectation. We see that during the last two hundred and fifty years the human mind has been in the highest degree active, that it had made great advances in every branch of natural philosophy, that it has produced innumerable inventions tending to promote the convenience of life, that medicine, surgery, chemistry, engineering, have been very greatly improved, that government, police, and law have been improved, though not to so great an extent as the physical sciences. But we see that, during these two hundred and fifty years, Protestantism has made no conquest worth speaking of. Nay, we believe that, as far as there has been a change, that change has, on the whole, been in favour of the Church of Rome. We cannot, therefore, feel confident

that the progress of knowledge will necessarily be fatal to a
system which has, to say the least, stood its ground in spite
of the immense progress made by the human race in knowledge since the days of Queen Elizabeth.'

*   *   *   *   *   *   *   *   *

'The history of Catholicism strikingly illustrates these ob-
servations. During the last seven centuries the public
mind of Europe has made constant progress in every department of secular knowledge. But in religion we can
trace no constant progress. The ecclesiastical history of
that period is a history of movement to and fro. Four
times, since the authority of the Church of Rome was established in Western Christendom, has the human intellect
risen up against her yoke. Twice that Church remained
completely victorious. Twice she came forth from the con-
flict bearing the marks of cruel wounds, but with the
principle of life still strong within her. When we reflect on
the tremendous assaults which she has survived, we find it
difficult to conceive in what way she is to perish.'

*   *   *   *   *   *   *   *   *

'It is impossible to deny that the polity of the Church of
Rome is the very masterpiece of human wisdom. In truth,
nothing but such a polity could, against such assaults, have
borne up such doctrines. The experience of twelve hundred eventful years, the ingenuity and patient care of forty
generations of statesmen, have improved that polity to such
perfection that, among the contrivances which have been
devised for deceiving and oppressing mankind, it occupies

the highest place. The stronger our conviction that reason and Scripture were decidedly on the side of Protestantism, the greater is the reluctant admiration with which we regard that system of tactics against which reason and Scripture were employed in vain.'

❊　＊　❊　❊　❊　　＊　＊　❊

' It is not strange that, in the year 1799, even sagacious observers should have thought that, at length, the hour of the Church of Rome was come. An infidel power ascendant, the Pope dying in captivity, the most illustrious prelates of France living in a foreign country on Protestant alms, the noblest edifices which the munificence of former ages had consecrated to the worship of God turned into temples of Victory, or into banqueting-houses for political societies, or into Theophilanthropic chapels, such signs might well be supposed to indicate the approaching end of that long domination.'

' But the end was not yet. Again doomed to death, the milk-white hind was still fated not to die. Even before the funeral rites had been performed over the ashes of Pius VI a great reaction had commenced which, after the lapse of more than forty years, appears to be still in progress. Anarchy had had its day. A new order of things rose out of the confusion, new dynasties, new laws, new titles, and amidst them, the ancient religion. The Arabs have a fable that the Great Pyramid was built by antediluvian kings, and alone, of all the works of men, bore the weight of the flood. Such as this was the fate of the Papacy. It had been buried under the great inundation ; but its deep foundations had remained unshaken ; and when the waters abated it appeared alone amidst the ruins of a world that had passed away. The Republic of Holland was gone, and the empire of Germany, and the great Council of Venice, and the old Helvetian League, and the House of Bourbon, and the parliaments and aristocracy of France. Europe was full of young creations : a French empire, a kingdom of Italy, a Confederation of the Rhine. Nor had the late events affected only territorial limits and political institutions. The distribution of property, the composition and spirit of society, had, through great part of Catholic Europe, undergone a complete change. But the unchangeable Church was still there.'

FINIS.